To Jean

Be made whole one.
And healthy in Jesus Name
Nancy 2017

SELAH

KIMBERLY DANIELS

CHARISMA
HOUSE

SELAH by Kimberly Daniels
Published by Charisma House
Charisma Media/Charisma House Book Group
600 Rinehart Road
Lake Mary, Florida 32746
www.charismahouse.com

Cover design by Justin Evans

Visit the author's website at www.kimberlydaniels.net.

Library of Congress Cataloging-in-Publication Data:
Names: Daniels, Kimberly, author.
Title: Selah / Kimberly Daniels.
Description: First edition. | Lake Mary, Florida : Charisma House, 2017. |
    Includes bibliographical references.
Identifiers: LCCN 2016045620| ISBN 9781629989693 (trade paper) | ISBN
    9781629989709 (ebook)
Subjects: LCSH: Devotional literature.
Classification: LCC BV4832.3 .D36 2017 | DDC 242--dc23
LC record available at https://lccn.loc.gov/2016045620

17 18 19 20 21 — 987654321
Printed in the United States of America

I dedicate this book to the late Dr. C. Peter Wagner.

When I first met Dr. Wagner, I was holding church services in a dilapidated building, and I had only about twelve mem-

bers. Yet he saw something in me that no one else could see. At that time I had never preached outside of Florida and had stood before only a few hundred people at the most. 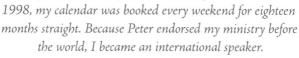 *But Dr. Wagner invited me to be a guest speaker at the International Conference on Deliverance in Colorado Springs, Colorado, and after that meeting in the summer of 1998, my calendar was booked every weekend for eighteen months straight. Because Peter endorsed my ministry before the world, I became an international speaker.*

I did not have a book when I spoke at the conference, but over the microphone, Peter said, "She will have a book!" Now, many books later, though Peter said he was not a prophet, I can attest to the fact that his words did not fall to the ground.

Peter, the apostolic movement will miss you. You have been a father to many and a general in the kingdom. Selah.

CONTENTS

INTRODUCTION

I T IS NO secret that I have faced some challenges over the past few years. During this time, as a way of encouraging myself and others, I posted my thoughts and revelations from God on my Kimberly Daniels public figure Facebook page and Periscope. The responses to the posts were so numerous that my publisher asked me to consider sharing in a book what I had posted. The result is what you are holding in your hands. We titled it *Selah* because that is the way I ended most of my posts.

The Hebrew word *Selah*, used many times in the Book of Psalms, means "pause and think on that." This book contains ninety daily meditational readings from a spiritual warfare perspective, written during the most difficult season I have ever walked through, that you can pause and think about. They are intended to provide you with daily encouragement and total spiritual breakthrough, particularly in the midst of tough times.

TROUBLE IS A BLESSING IN DISGUISE

And the Lord restored the fortunes of Job when he prayed for his friends, and also the Lord gave Job twice as much as he had before.

—Job 42:10

Gᴏᴅ ɪꜱ ɢᴏɪɴɢ to give you double for your trouble. In Job 42 the Bible says the Lord not only restored the fortunes of Job but also gave him twice as much as he had before. His latter days were more blessed than his beginning (Job 42:12). The pain and the hardship Job went through set him up for a double portion of God's blessing.

God doesn't allow trouble for trouble's sake. If you're going through a hard season right now, read Job 42. Your suffering is not in vain. God is a restorer. He will give you double for your trouble. *Selah.*

Today pray...

> Lord, I pray that You will help me see that the trouble that comes into my life is not just trouble for trouble's sake but a chance for me to receive a double portion of Your blessing. I declare the blessing of Job over my life right now in the name of Jesus. My time of suffering has not been in vain. You will restore to me everything that has been lost—and then some! In Jesus's name, amen.

_____

_____

_____

_____

_____

_____

_____

_____

_____

_____

_____

_____

_____

_____

_____

_____

_____

_____

_____

_____

_____

_____

_____

_____

PEOPLE NEED MORE THAN INFORMATION

For the kingdom of God is not in word, but in power.
—1 CORINTHIANS 4:20

NE NIGHT I had a dream that some men broke into my house and were after my family. They were too powerful for me to fight, so I ran out of the house to get help. I ran to a phone booth and dialed 911. When the operator answered, she said, "This is directory assistance. May I help you?"

In frustration I told the operator that I had an emergency and needed 911, but I must have dialed 411 by mistake. I dialed 911 again, and the operator offered me directory assistance a second time. *Really* frustrated this time, I boldly told the person on the other line, "I'm facing a life-and-death situation. I don't need information; I need help!"

This was a prophetic dream that exposed a problem in the church. People are coming to the church for help, but preachers are giving them just information. They are dialing 911 and getting 411. The kingdom of God is not just in word but also in *power*! People need to experience the power of God that brings deliverance. *Selah.*

Today pray . . .

> *Lord, I ask that You will allow me to see the needs
> of others and be ready to help. You have chosen me
> to be Your hands and feet for such a time as this.*

Let me be ready to be all things to all men when that time comes. Thank You, God, for blessing me to be a blessing. In Jesus's name, amen.

_____

_____

_____

_____

_____

_____

_____

_____

_____

_____

_____

_____

_____

_____

_____

_____

_____

_____

GOD GIVES THE INCREASE

I have planted, Apollos watered, but God gave the increase.
—1 Corinthians 3:6

ONE DAY MY twins were taking a picture of the trees in my front yard. You have to look close to see it, but there is a small tree on the left side of a bigger tree. Both were planted when the twins were five years old, but one tree grew tall and the other stayed small. Both trees had the same sun, received the same water, and were planted in the same ground—good ground—yet only one grew big.

As I was looking at those trees that day, the Lord quickened my spirit concerning increase. He said, "One will plant, another will water, but only God can bring *increase!*" (See 1 Corinthians 3:6.) I believe that is a word to those who are discouraged because they have been comparing themselves to others.

What God has for you is for you. Stop comparing yourself to people who have a different lot in life. We will not all have the same portion in life.

Both trees in my front yard have what God put inside them. Even though one is big and the other is small, each one is what He called it to be. The fact that one tree is bigger does not mean it is better. Big things come in small packages.

I pastor a church in Jacksonville, Florida. Is my church a big church? It depends on what I stand it next to or compare it with. To the mega-ministries, my church is small. To the storefront churches, it's big! I thank God for my portion! No matter the size, it's all right with me.

Be encouraged! Thank God for your lot in life and praise Him for your portion. If you compare where you are in life or ministry to the portion God has promised you, then you can never fail. "Thank God for the increase He has already given you in life, and new doors of abundance will be your portion," says the Lord of hosts. Amen.

Today pray...

> *Father God, I thank You for my lot in life and praise You for my portion. As I compare my ministry only to the portion You have promised me, I know I cannot fail. I thank You for the increase You have already given me and new doors of abundance that will be opened unto me. In the name of Jesus I pray. Amen.*

JOY TO THE WORLD

My brothers, count it all joy when you fall into diverse temptations,
knowing that the trying of your faith develops patience.
—JAMES 1:2—3

THE WORLD NEEDS joy. So many people are suicidal and depressed, especially around the holidays. Somehow people convince themselves that their lives are horrible when they are actually better than the picture they have drawn for themselves. The Bible clearly gives hope that we can have joy in whatever season we are facing in life. James 1:2 says that even in the midst of all kinds of trials, we can count it all joy.

Joy is the answer to every problem, and it is an outflow of the Holy Spirit in our lives. The Bible tells us in Galatians 5:22–23 that the fruit of the Spirit is love, joy, peace, faithfulness, kindness, gentleness, patience, goodness, and self-control. When the Holy Spirit is overflowing in your life, His fruit will be evident. If you're anything like me, seeing that list lets you know you need more of the Holy Spirit. That's OK. You can receive a fresh infilling of the Holy Spirit right now. Just repent of your sins and shortcomings and let Him fill you up until you overflow.

Once your heart is right with God, do not be afraid to ask Him for what you want. If you need more joy, ask for it. John 16:24 says, "Ask, and you will receive, that your joy may be full."

I speak fullness of joy over you right now. And I encourage you to stop worrying about the plans and plots evil people are making against you. Proverbs 10:28 says your hope brings joy, but the expectations of the wicked will perish. Every evil expectation against you will be shut down before it leaves your enemy's mind.

All of creation has your back. You shall go out in joy and be led forth in peace. The mountains the enemy has put before you shall turn and attack him and then break forth in singing. And the trees of the field shall clap for you. (See Isaiah 55:12.) The Creator and all He has created is cheering for you.

I come against depression and suicide in Jesus's name. If you have sown in tears, you will reap in joy (Ps. 126:5). May you endure everything with perseverance and patience joyfully (Col. 1:11). The joy of the Lord is your strength (Neh. 8:10).

Today declare…

> *The joy of the Lord is my strength, and the peace of God goes before me. I declare that every evil expectation set against me today will be shut down in Jesus's name. No weapon formed against me will prosper. I am strong in the Lord and in the power of His might!*

_____

_____

_____

_____

_____

_____

FULLNESS OF JOY

*You will make known to me the path of life; in Your presence is
fullness of joy; at Your right hand there are pleasures for evermore.*
—PSALM 16:11

PSALM 16:11 SHOWS us the path of life and declares that
in the presence of the Lord there is fullness of joy. On
the other hand, when we're around an evil presence, there is
heaviness, confusion, depression, and the release of thought
patterns that lead to death.

Don't allow people with bad spirits to follow you. They
will suck the joy out of you.

Psalm 27:6 says you can have joy even in the midst of your
enemies. Hold your head up and never let the haters see you
looking down. Your help comes from the Lord. And He is
not down below. If you want to find God, look up! The devil
is the one under your feet.

I know it's been a long night, but weeping endures only for
the night (Ps. 30:5). If you can just make it to the morning,
you will be all right. *Joy comes in the morning!*

Today declare...

> *Morning is here, and I will be full of joy in the
> presence of the Lord. I hold my head up in the
> midst of my enemies because the Lord is my helper.
> No heaviness, confusion, or depression will have its
> way in my life, in Jesus's name.*

_____

_____

_____

_____

_____

_____

_____

_____

_____

_____

_____

_____

_____

_____

_____

_____

_____

_____

_____

_____

_____

ARE YOU SATISFIED IN HIM?

*You satisfy me more than the richest feast. I
will praise you with songs of joy.*

—PSALM 63:5, NLT

❧

JOY IS AN emotional manifestation evoked by exceptionally
good or satisfying results in one's life. The key word here
is *satisfying* results.

When I think of the word *satisfied*, the first thing I think
of is a debt being paid off. Jesus paid the ultimate price when
He died for our sins. The devil put us in debt, but Jesus came
and paid it off. A concern I have with believers is that some
of them are *saved* and even *sanctified*, but I question whether
they are truly *satisfied*!

The second thing that comes to my mind concerning this
powerful word *satisfied* is the idea of "being full." The word
satisfied literally means to be filled to capacity until there is
room for nothing else. For example, if I have three houses to
visit for Christmas dinner, the first house visited will get most
of my attention because I'm hungry. The last two houses will
get whatever I have left over. And if I eat too much and have
no room for more, I will not be interested in eating anymore
at the last house because I will already be full.

I can still go and hang out at another house after I am full,
but I will not be able to accomplish the purpose for which I
was invited—to eat—because I have already been satisfied
and have no room for more. The Bible says that we should
"taste and see that the LORD is good" (Ps. 34:8). When our

bellies are filled with life's challenges, there is no room for God. That's why the only way He can show up and show out in our lives is if we put Him first! Matthew 6:33 tells us to seek the kingdom of God first, and then everything we need will be given to us.

I have come to the conclusion that many people are depressed and suicidal because they do not have Jesus in their lives. They go to work and through their everyday activities "faking it till they make it." This is less than what God has planned for our lives.

Joy is not a secular word. It was created from the heart of God. People can have fun or feel good, but they can get joy only from God. His joy is our strength! If we attempt to get joy from anything else, something will always be missing. No joy, no power! I'm not speaking of having power to do miracles or to move mountains but having the power simply to think straight.

With all the troubles of the times we live in, people need power to have peace of mind. Some need power just to have the desire to wake up in the morning. Powerless people often manifest the following:

+ Hatred	+ Bitterness	+ Defamation
+ Jealousy	+ Unforgiveness	of character
+ Envy	+ Competitiveness	and other
+ Strife	+ Negativity	forms of
+ Slander	+ Gossip	verbal abuse

Unfortunately miserable people specialize in making others miserable. A person with no joy is like a walking volcano about to erupt. This eruption will flow over into the lives of those with whom they come in contact. They have a darkness about them that is contagious, and they are definitely not fun to be with. This is not what God wants for His people.

Finally, a person with no joy is never satisfied and is always needy. Trying to help a person like this can be toilsome. The more you do for him, the more you end up having to do for him. Helping a person with no joy is like putting your time and efforts in a bag with holes in it because he has no ability to receive or hold on to what he is given.

So I ask you, are you really satisfied? I'm not judging; I'm just asking! If by chance you are not satisfied, let me ask you this: Whose house have you been eating at that has caused you to have no more room for God? The reason God does not want us to put things before Him is that He does not like leftovers. Leftovers are good for Thanksgiving and Christmas, but God requires our first love.

In the midst of our busy days, if we don't stop by His house first, we will have no room left in our lives for Him. God says that putting anything before Him is idolatry. *Selah.* Pause and think on that.

If you are suffering from rejection, hurt, depression, difficulties in life, or suicidal thoughts, dedicate or rededicate your heart to God. Only He can turn your mourning to *joy*!

Pray with me…

> *Father God, in the name of Jesus, I dedicate (rededicate) my heart to You. Take out this stony heart and give me a heart of flesh. I renounce the cares of this world and cast my cares on You. Save me, deliver me, and fill me with Your Holy Spirit. I surrender all to Your lordship. Amen.*

_____

_____

_____

_____

_____

_____

_____

_____

_____

_____

_____

_____

_____

_____

_____

_____

_____

_____

_____

_____

_____

_____

_____

_____

PUT YOUR TRUST IN GOD, AND REJOICE!

But may all those who seek refuge in You rejoice; may they ever shout for joy, because You defend them; may those who love Your name be joyful in You.

—PSALM 5:11

PSALM 5:11 SAYS that those who put their trust in God should always rejoice and shout for joy because He is their defense. It also says the people who love the name of the Lord should be joyful in Him. The name of the Lord is a strong tower; the righteous run into it and they are safe (Prov. 18:10).

We know that Jesus is the name above every name, but there are many names for God in the Old Testament. At midnight on New Year's Eve I am always somewhere shut in declaring the power of the names of God into my year. I know the coming year will be one of tests and trials, but those trials will lead to much victory for those who know who they are in the Holy Ghost. On the other hand, those who depend on their natural resources and abilities will fail.

Attempting to go back to the manna of previous years will cause you to suffer a spiritual deficit in your life. What worked in years past will spoil and dry up in the years to come. God is saying, "Move forward today!"

Do not resolve to do tomorrow what you can do today.

Today is the acceptable day of salvation. It is a day that the Lord has made. Rejoice and be glad in it!

Daniel 11:23 says the people who know their God will be strong and do great exploits. Do you know your God? Do you know who He really is? If you ever want to get to know God's nature and character, just take a look at what He calls Himself. We can put our confidence in who He declares Himself to be through His names. Consider the attributes found in the names of God listed below, which I included in my book *Inside Out*[1]:

+ *El Nosei*—the God Who Forgives (Ps. 99:8)
+ *Lechem Ha Chayim*—Bread of Life (John 6:48)
+ *Rosh Pinnah*—Capstone (Ps. 118:22)
+ *Peleh Yoetz*—Wonderful Counselor (Isa. 9:6)
+ *Boreh Ketzot Ha-Aretz*—Creator of the Ends of the Earth (Isa. 40:28)
+ *Zero 'ot Olam*—Everlasting Arms (Deut. 33:27)
+ *Melech Olam*—Eternal King (Jer. 10:10)
+ *Aviad*—Everlasting Father (Isa. 9:6)
+ *El Olam*—Everlasting God (Gen. 21:33)
+ *Avi*—Father (Ps. 89:26)
+ *Elohim Elyon*—God Most High (Ps. 57:2)
+ *Elohei Kol Nechaman*—God of All Comfort (2 Cor. 1:3)
+ *Elohei Kol Chen V'Chesed*—God of all Grace (1 Pet. 5:10)
+ *Elohei Kol Basar*—God of All Mankind (Jer. 32:27)

+ *Seh Elohim*—Lamb of God (John 1:29)
+ *Ohr Yisrael*—Light of Israel (Isa. 10:17)
+ *Ohr Ha Olam*—Light of the World (John 8:12)
+ *El Chai*—Living God (Ps. 84:2)
+ *Adonai*—Lord (Exod. 6:3)
+ *Adonai Nissi*—the Lord Is My Banner (Exod. 17:15)
+ *Adonai Echad O'shmo Echad*—Lord Is One (Zech. 14:9)
+ *Abba Avinul*—Father Our Father (Rom. 8:15)
+ *Yotzer Hakol*—Maker of All Things (Jer. 10:16)
+ *El Gibbor*—Mighty God (Isa. 9:6)
+ *Haggo'el*—Redeemer (Isa. 41:14)
+ *Ma'on*—Our Dwelling Place (Ps. 90:1)
+ *Esh Okhlah*—Consuming Fire (Deut. 4:24)
+ *Sar Shalom*—Prince of Peace (Isa. 9:6)
+ *Go'el Haddam*—Avenger of Blood (1 Sam. 6:20)
+ *Ro'eh*—Shepherd (Ps. 23:1)
+ *Ruach El*—Spirit of God (Job 33:4)
+ *Migdal Oz*—Strong Tower (Prov. 18:10)
+ *Elohim Emet*—True God (Jer. 10:10)
+ *Yashar*—Upright One (Isa. 26:7)
+ *Dvar Elohim*—Word of God (Rev. 19:13)
+ *Peleh*—Wonderful (Isa. 9:6)
+ *El Roi*—The God Who Sees Me (Gen. 16:13)
+ *Yah*—Yah (Ps. 68:4)

If you want to do great exploits for God, you need to know your God. Get to know Him—*really* know Him—by declaring the attributes of His names. As you come to know who He is, you'll also discover who you are in Him.

Today pray...

> *Lord, I thank You for who You are. You are faithful and never fail. I put my trust in Your name. I rejoice in Your name. I shout for joy because of who You are, God. Your name is above all other names. I praise Your name and lift it high. Your name is a strong tower to which I can run and where I know I am safe. Amen.*

THE CHOSEN FAST

*Is not this the fast that I have chosen: to loose the bonds
of wickedness, to undo the heavy burdens, and to let
the oppressed go free, and break every yoke?*

—ISAIAH 58:6

W HEN YOU DECIDE to fast, it is important to do the fast
that God has chosen for you.

Because I am a pastor, I am under another level of account-ability when it comes to seeking God for a fast that will break yokes through the corporate anointing in my church and through ministry affiliations. In 2014 the Lord spoke to me concerning the number five, a number that represents grace. I sensed that He was releasing grace on behalf of His people in 2015.

The consecration we did at Spoken Word Ministries at the beginning of 2015 was to consume only liquids for the first five days of the month for the first five months of the year. The fast started at 5:00 a.m. and ended at 5:00 p.m. every day. At midnight on New Year's Day we declared the names of God, releasing the power of who He is in the earth realm.

As we sought God through prayer and fasting, one of our prayer targets was to pray (with a sincere heart) for those who spitefully used us and operated as outright enemies. When Job prayed for those who came against him, God turned his captivity and set him free. We believed God would do the same in our lives—and He did. The Holy Spirit moved mightily in our church. We even received testimonies of breakthrough from people who weren't part of Spoken Word but who joined in the fast through Facebook and Twitter.

If you're in bondage because people have wronged you, seek God for His chosen fast. You may even want to consider following our fast from 2015. If you seek Him in fasting and prayer, God will bring breakthrough in your life.

Today pray…

> *Lord, I commit to Your chosen fast. I desire to see the bonds of wickedness broken over my life and the lives of those You have given me a burden to war for. I decree that every heavy burden will be lifted and every yoke broken, in Jesus's name. I pray for those who have spitefully used me and who have set themselves as enemies against me. I declare that as I pray for my enemies, I will be released from any bondage that has been formed as a result of wrongs against me, in the name of Jesus. Amen.*

_____

_____

_____

_____

_____

_____

_____

_____

_____

IT'S TIME TO UN-COMMIT

To everything there is a season, a time for every purpose under heaven . . . a time to cast away stones, and a time to gather stones; a time to embrace, and a time to refrain from embracing; a time to gain, and a time to lose; a time to keep, and a time to cast away.

—ECCLESIASTES 3:1–6

A GOOD WAY TO gauge what holds weight in your life is to examine how you spend your time from midnight until noon on New Year's Eve. It will reveal "who's who" in your life.

You need to be clear about what your real commitments are. You need to be clear on what church and pastor you are committed to, what job assignments you are committed to, and even what family, friends, and close relationships you are committed to. It doesn't matter who makes the list or why.

Once you realize what you are committed to, you must be ready to un-commit. There are some people, places, and things that will hinder the flow of the Holy Spirit in your life and keep you from setting the right priorities. In the name of Jesus, un-commit them! Old things have passed away. Allow God to make things *new*.

Sometimes it is hard to cut out old things because they have become habits. Identify the old habits that are trying to come into the next season with you. Admit it: you know that behavior or that relationship isn't working, but you continue to entertain it because it has become a habit. Let it go! The Bible speaks of the old man. This old man (or old attitude) will ride your back as long as you give him permission. Drop him off and never let him get on your back again!

People, places, and things that have been a problem for you in the past will probably be a problem for you in the future unless you let them go. So make a decision today—out with the old and in with the new!

Today pray...

> *Lord, I pray that as I enter this next season of life I will be wise and discerning to know who is with me and who is not, what habits I need to let go of and what new habits I need to start. Help me to identify the things in my life that are not in line with Your plans for me. I commit to un-commit to whatever does not fit and is no longer working for my good. I am ready to walk into this new season victorious and free. In Jesus's name, amen.*

_____

_____

_____

_____

_____

_____

_____

_____

_____

KNOW YOUR TRUE FRIENDS

*For it is not an enemy who reproaches me; then I could
bear it. Nor is it one who hates me who has exalted himself
against me; then I could hide from him. But it was you, my
peer, my guide, and my acquaintance. We took pleasant counsel
together, and walked to the house of God in company.*

—PSALM 55:12–14

PEOPLE WHO LOVE you and have your best interest at
heart will never connect themselves with people who
are at odds with you. If someone you consider a friend
continually associates with your enemies, do not be ignorant
of this device of the enemy. A true friend *never* gives his ear
to your accusers.

And be careful when someone confronts you about what
"they" said. (Who are "they," anyway?) Whoever "they" are,
you are better off without them! *Selah.*

Today pray…

*Father God, I pray that You will help me know
who my true friends are. Your Word says that a
true friend is one who sticks closer than a brother
(Prov. 18:24). I know that even if my mother and
father were to betray me, You would be close beside
me. So God, I pray for wisdom and discernment as
I seek out the people You want me to have in my
life. I declare that they will be for me as You are for
me. In Jesus's name, amen.*

_____

_____

_____

_____

_____

_____

_____

_____

_____

_____

_____

_____

_____

_____

_____

_____

_____

_____

_____

_____

_____

FRENEMIES

The LORD said to my lord, "Sit at My right hand,
until I make your enemies your footstool."

—PSALM 110:1

D O NOT FRET over "frenemies." Allow God to make your enemies your footstool.

A footstool is used for two main reasons: to prop your feet up or to help you reach what you cannot get with your natural height. Allow God to let people who plot evil against you help you get to your next level. Without Judas, Jesus could not have gotten to the cross.

While you are in the twilight of your next level or transitioning into it, that footstool will be there for you to prop your feet on if you understand its purpose. There is no promotion without persecution and no testimony without a test.

Praise God for the footstools in your life. These frenemies may think they are slick, but God is the one laughing. *Selah.* Pause and think on that.

Today declare…

> *There is no promotion without persecution. Lord,*
> *I praise You for making my enemies my footstool.*

_____

_____

_____

THE ANSWER TO EVERYTHING

Money answereth all things.
—Ecclesiastes 10:19, KJV

Money answers all things when you have God. When you don't have God, money will put a big question mark over your head. Having money with no favor is a curse because true favor exists only in God. This is why as Christians we achieve much with little, because God will add His super to our natural and show up and show out on our behalf. The Scripture is true: those who are faithful over little will eventually rule over much (Luke 16:10).

God is raising up the underdog. If you are the last, get ready to be the first. If the status quo is against you, you have a lot working for you. Read Judges 6 and 7. God is raising up the Gideons of society—the ones who think they are the lowest and the least—to deal with the Midianites who have been taking our prosperity. *Selah.* Pause and think on that.

Today declare...

> *The Lord is adding His super to my natural, and He is taking my faithfulness in the little things and making me ruler over much.*

STABBED IN THE BACK

You will be hated by all men for My name's sake. But
he who endures to the end will be saved.

—MATTHEW 10:22

I HAVE BEEN GETTING many Macedonian calls from the Holy Spirit to reach out to people who have been stabbed in the back by the people they least expected to hurt them. If you have an ear and that describes you, hear what God is saying to you today.

Stop crying, shake yourself, and hold your head up high. Think about it. Who are you that people are taking the time to set you up? I can answer that question. You must be all that! People can't sleep at night because they're jealous that you are so blessed. Their soft pillows have become stones. They cannot move forward because God has made their way hard.

Hard hearts create hard beds and hard ways. Make sure your heart is right and that resentment, bitterness, and unforgiveness (the threefold cord that brings death to your joy) do not penetrate the perimeters of your peace.

Remember this: the religious leaders hated Jesus. One day you will have to come to grips with the fact that if you have any God in you, you *will* be hated too!

When people who do not know you fight you, your defense is putting on the whole armor of God. But when people who are familiar with you fight you, turn to God and guard your heart! *Selah.*

Today pray…

> *Lord, I submit my heart to You. Search me and let me know if any resentment, bitterness, or unforgiveness has set in. Put a guard around my heart and make Your peace an impenetrable wall against the enemies of my soul. In Jesus's name, amen.*

_____

_____

_____

_____

_____

_____

_____

_____

_____

_____

_____

_____

_____

_____

_____

CHOOSE THE BLESSING

I have set before you life and death, blessing and curse. Therefore
choose life, that both you and your descendants may live.

—DEUTERONOMY 30:19

CURSES GO BACK three or four generations, but blessings go forward for a thousand generations. (See Exodus 20:5–6.) You cannot change the negative things that have occurred in your bloodline, but as Paul did, you can press toward the mark of the high calling. The high calling is blessing. God has ordained that your generations be blessed.

For all the mothers and fathers who have children on the wrong track, have you ever thought they may be plagued with the mistakes of your past or the mistakes of your ancestors? This is not just some spooky theory. Generational curses are real. The good news is that it's not too late. You can take authority over the destiny of your seed. How? Start by making the right choices now! Everything you do today will affect your children tomorrow.

Yes, the curses go back four generations, but the blessings go forward for a thousand. Choose the blessing for your bloodline, and the curse will be broken.

Make this confession:

> *Father God, in the name of Jesus, I repent of every*
> *bad choice I made that has influence on the destiny*
> *of my seed. I declare that every mishap, misfortune,*
> *and mistake is under the blood. No weapons*

formed against me, my children, my children's children, or any of the generations to follow will prosper. Every tongue that has risen against our purpose has no power. Lord, I thank You. I choose the blessing and renounce the curse. In Jesus's name, amen.

_____

_____

_____

_____

_____

_____

_____

_____

_____

_____

_____

_____

_____

_____

_____

_____

DO NOT LET YOUR ACCUSERS PUT OUT YOUR LIGHT

You are the light of the world. A city that is set on a hill cannot be hidden. Neither do men light a candle and put it under a basket, but on a candlestick. And it gives light to all who are in the house. Let your light so shine before men that they may see your good works and glorify your Father who is in heaven.

—MATTHEW 5:14–16

No MATTER WHAT our fleshly shortcomings are—even on our best day our righteousness is as filthy rags—we are still children of the light. A little light dispels the greatest darkness. This is why the enemies of God get confused. Every time they do evil against you, God takes the arrow, makes it a boomerang, and turns the situation around for your good.

Walk in the light. Arise and shine because your light has come. And when light comes, darkness must flee. Be encouraged and do not let your accusers put out your light. The only reason they hate you is because they really admire you and want to be just like you. You are *all that* to them because you are filled with light.

Share that light with someone today and make a difference in the world. Be a shaker and a mover! Shake the devil off and move in the things of God.

The twin to joy is peace. There is nothing like peace! There is no joy without peace. It is the armor that causes weapons that are formed against you to *never* prosper. Like water rolls off a duck's back, peace causes the greatest torpedo to melt in your presence—because you're in His presence.

Today declare...

> *My accusers will not put out my light. I will arise and shine!*

_____

_____

_____

_____

_____

_____

_____

_____

_____

_____

_____

_____

_____

_____

CHANGING SEASONS

While the earth remains, seedtime and harvest, cold and heat, summer and winter, and day and night will not cease.

—Genesis 8:22

THOSE WHO HAVE a revelation of the spirit know that whenever the seasons change in the natural, a change is also happening in the spirit. With spring comes the spring equinox. In the summer there is the summer solstice and then in the fall the autumn equinox. In December the change of the season is called the winter solstice.

Solstice relates to the sun and *equinox* to the moon. Evil people use these times to attempt to demonically manipulate things in the earth realm. If you believe only what you see in the natural, you won't get this because the natural mind cannot discern the things of the spirit.

As people of prayer, our assignment is to break the power of the demonic seeds planted in the atmosphere because those seeds are meant to produce evil fruit that will hinder what God wants to do in the earth realm. The devil has only the power we give him. Jesus has all power, and He was gracious enough to give it to us.

The Bible says the sons of Issachar were men who knew the times and what Israel should do (1 Chron. 12:32). It is time to recognize the times and seasons, and what God would have us do to protect the promise He has given us. Victory is in your hands. Exercise the power you have been

given over the enemy and root out demonic seeds so they
cannot produce fruit.

Today declare...

> *No weapon formed against me will prosper. I root*
> *out every demonic seed and declare that it shall not*
> *bring forth fruit. The purposes of God will prevail.*
> *No demon in hell will break the power of the seeds*
> *God has planted in my life. In Jesus's name, amen.*

_____

_____

_____

_____

_____

_____

_____

_____

_____

_____

_____

_____

_____

YOUR SUCCESS DEFEATS HATERS

You prepare a table before me in the presence of my enemies;
You anoint my head with oil; my cup runs over.
—PSALM 23:5

BELIEVERS, YOU HAVE power over those who plan evil against you. The best way to defeat your enemies is to do great exploits for God. Greatness is in you because the Greater One is in you. Faith without works is dead. Put boots to the ground and be all God has called you to be. Your success through Christ defeats your haters.

I declare achievement and success over your life and command every demonic seedling assigned against you to dry up in the ground in which it was planted. I declare that you will not be depressed, financially overwhelmed, confused, distracted, disappointed, or stuck in limbo.

The demonic prince over your situation has been displaced. It's time for you to walk in great victory! *Selah.*

Today declare…

> *I will put boots to the ground and be all that God*
> *has called me to be because the Greater One is in me.*

_____

_____

_____

_____

_____

_____

_____

_____

_____

_____

_____

_____

_____

_____

_____

_____

_____

_____

_____

_____

_____

_____

_____

A WORD TO THE MOVERS AND SHAKERS

... one chase a thousand, and two put ten thousand to flight ...
—DEUTERONOMY 32:30

WHEN YOU HAVE what it takes, people will attempt to take what you have so they can get what they need. Movers and shakers cannot surround themselves with needy or greedy people. If you are trying to move up or on in life, you can go only as high or as far as the people you surround yourself with.

My favorite scripture is that one person can put a thousand to flight but two (representing the double portion) can put ten thousand to flight. The wrong partnerships will bring you down, but the right partnerships will cause you to put the enemy to flight. *Selah.*

Today pray ...

> *Lord, lead me to the right associations so that I may form partnerships that will put the enemy to flight and that I may go higher in what You have planned for my life. In Jesus's name, I pray. Amen.*

_____

_____

_____

_____

_____

_____

_____

_____

_____

_____

_____

_____

_____

_____

_____

_____

_____

_____

_____

_____

_____

_____

_____

_____

_____

_____

THE POWER OF PRAISE
AND WORSHIP MUSIC

*It happened that when the evil spirit from God came on Saul,
David would take the lyre in his hand and play. So Saul was
refreshed and was well, and the evil spirit departed from him.*

—1 Samuel 16:23

My twin boys have been sleeping to praise and
worship music since they were in my womb. Since
they were little boys their favorite artists have been Grace
Williams, who often sings at Benny Hinn crusades, and
Kathy Summers Kelley of Crusaders Church in Chicago.
One morning as I walked into one of my twin boys' rooms,
I heard that my son had Maranatha! and Hosanna! worship
music playing. Yes, if you raise them in the way they should
go, *they will not depart!*

God moves through praise and worship music even while
we're sleeping. If you listen to praise and worship music
while you sleep, you can even receive deliverance. You don't
believe me? When David played his musical instrument,
Saul was relieved of the demonic spirits that tormented
him. But his relief was always temporary because his heart
was not right. If he had been willing to repent, his change
would have been lasting.

Praise and worship and repentance open the door to great
peace and uninterrupted power in the Holy Ghost. *Selah.*

Today pray . . .

> *Lord, I pray that my worship to You is a sweet fragrance in Your nostrils. Let my praise, worship, and heart of repentance open the door to great peace in my life. May the power of the Holy Spirit flood my life without interruption. In Jesus's name, amen.*

_____

_____

_____

_____

_____

_____

_____

_____

_____

_____

_____

_____

_____

_____

_____

TAKE TIME WITH THOSE WHO LOVE YOU

*Let us not forsake the assembling of ourselves together, as
is the manner of some, but let us exhort one another,
especially as you see the Day approaching.*

—HEBREWS 10:25

ONE WEEK WHEN I was very busy, my puppy kept
getting in my way. I had to keep scolding him because
every time I took a step he was under my feet. I kept putting
him in his crate because I did not have time to play with him.
Then one day when I woke up, instead of trying to be under
me, he just sat there looking at me.

That day I realized something very important: whatever
or whomever you take for granted may not always continue
to be there for you when you get time for them. When you
finally get time, they may be uninterested or gone.

I made time to give my puppy some attention. I realized
it is a blessing for him to covet my attention. It is a blessing
to have people in your life who love you. Make time to honor
them. *Selah.*

Today declare…

> *I will honor those who love me. I will make time
> for the ones I love.*

ADONAI!

*I have said to the LORD, "You are my Lord; my
welfare has no existence outside of You."*

—PSALM 16:2

—⟡—

I WAS DRIVING ONE night when I received a message that
there had been three gunshot situations in a matter
of two hours. Two young ladies were killed. Despite the
circumstances, the next morning I woke up with peace in my
heart, and I heard the Holy Spirit tell me, "Adonai."

Many people can relate to Jesus as Savior—we receive
His salvation by the confession of our mouths and what
we believe in our hearts. But He is more than that. *Adonai*
is a plural word in the Hebrew, and it means "Lord, Lord,
Lord!"[1] Jesus is our Savior, and He is our Lord.

The Hebrew word *adon* also means "lord" but in another
sense. It is the word Sarah used when she called Abraham
"my lord" (Gen. 18:3, 12). He was lord with the lowercase *l*.
But Adonai is Lord of lords, or "Lord, Lord, Lord."

This lordship manifests in our everyday life. It's not just
something we talk about or something we think about; it's
something we live. The Lord God is all-powerful, and He
intervenes in our lives on a daily basis.

If you do not see Adonai intervening in your everyday
affairs, it may be because you need to shift to allow Him
to have His way in your life. Maybe you need to surrender
completely to His control. Sometimes we think we are
waiting on God, but He is actually waiting on us.

The blessings of the Lord will run you down and take you over. Stop running after the blessing. Slow down and bask in the favor of Adonai. When He is Lord in your life and your ways please Him, even your enemies will be at peace with you. *Selah!*

Today declare...

> *Lord, I receive the revelation of Adonai. Manifest Your lordship in my life today.*

_____

_____

_____

_____

_____

_____

_____

_____

_____

_____

_____

_____

_____

_____

LET GOD CHANGE YOUR NAME

*No longer will your name be called Abram, but your name will be
Abraham, for I have made you the father of a multitude of nations.*

—GENESIS 17:5

SOMETIMES BEFORE HE can shift your game and take
you to the next level He has for you, God has to change
your name. God had to change Abram's name to Abraham,
Sarai's name to Sarah, Jacob's name to Israel, and Simon's
name to Peter. Abraham went from "exalted father" to
"father of a multitude" (Gen. 17:5). Sarah went from "my
princess" to "mother of nations" (Gen. 17:15). Jacob/Israel
went from "supplanter" to "having power with God" (Gen.
32:28), and Peter went from "God has heard" to "rock" (John
1:42). Their old names didn't match what God had in store
for them.

Don't get caught up in what people have called you. "Failure,"
"depressed," or "defeated" may have described you in the past,
but God is still in the business of changing names. In Christ
you are now "victorious," "joyful," and "an overcomer."

I prophesy that you are ripe for picking and you are in
place to be shifted to your next level. You have been called
and ordained, and you cannot lose with the gifts you use.
Do not weary yourself over people who attempt to tear you
down. If they did not build you up, they cannot tear you
down! Except God build a thing, the people labor in vain.
What He has for you, the chosen, cannot be stopped. *Selah.*

Today declare...

> *I am ripe for the picking. I am in place to be shifted to my next level. What God has chosen for me cannot be stopped.*

_____

_____

_____

_____

_____

_____

_____

_____

_____

_____

_____

_____

_____

_____

_____

_____

_____

WIN WITH LOVE

*Above all things, have unfailing love for one another,
because love covers a multitude of sins.*

—1 PETER 4:8

～♒～

PASTOR CLINT BROWN wrote a song called "I Win" that I have listened to over and over. It says that no matter what weapon is formed against you, you win. I love that song—it makes me want to dance—and it also has a powerful spiritual connotation.

The Bible says that no weapon formed against you will prosper (Isa. 54:17), and trust me, those weapons do form. I recently had a dream in which I saw a lady who I thought was my friend at the water working witchcraft against me. She was also nailing my name to a tree, cursing me. I pray for that woman and have encouraged others to do the same because I saw the spiritual manipulation she worked against me turning and causing her to be bedridden.

Despite what I saw in that dream, I still love her. The real power of God resides in the love we show those who spitefully come against us. This woman suffers from extreme depression, and it causes her heart to be filled with deep-seated hatred. The love of God is her only hope.

At the places where I travel to speak and on social media sites, people always ask me how to deal with attacks. Here's my response: love covers a multitude of sins.

When you take the position to love your enemies, it disarms them. Do not retaliate, and God will expedite your blessing. Your enemies will scatter, and the weapon used against you will misfire and malfunction. It will roll off like water off a duck's back. I'm so glad there is no power that can compare to the power of the blood of my Lord Jesus. *Selah.*

Today declare...

> *I take up my position to love my enemies. I win with love.*

LIVING IN GENERATIONAL BLESSINGS

*His offspring shall be mighty in the land; the
generation of the upright shall be blessed.*

—Psalm 112:2

M Y DADDY, ANDREW Preston Perkins, ran for city
council many times, but to no avail. My dad was a
voice in the black community during times of great disparity.
But I was young at the time and did not pay the political
scene any attention. Now as a former city council member I
realize that I am living the manifestation of his dream. God
allowed me to go where my dad wanted to go.

The generational blessings are stronger than the curses.
The Bible says family curses go back three or four generations,
but family blessings *go forward* for a thousand generations
(Exod. 20:5–6). God ordained that I should walk in political
office, just as God ordained that Solomon, not his father,
David, should build the temple. God has a blessing ordained
for you too. Ask Him to show you what family blessing you
are supposed to call forth in your life or pass on to the next
generation. It's time to live in generational blessing! *Selah.*

Today pray…

> *God, I thank You that I am living the manifestation
> of the dreams of those who have gone before me.
> Thank You for allowing me to go into places they*

could only dream about. I declare, Lord, that the generational blessings in my family line are stronger than the curses. Continue to bless me to go further and further in You. In Jesus's name, amen.

_____

_____

_____

_____

_____

_____

_____

_____

_____

_____

_____

_____

_____

_____

_____

_____

_____

_____

DWELL IN THE LAND
OF INTEGRITY

If you are willing and obedient, you shall eat the good of the land.
—ISAIAH 1:19

❧

BE VERY CAREFUL what you find pleasure in. I take pleasure in being a child of the King, an heir of God, and a joint heir with Christ. My pleasure is in my God.

There are two kinds of pleasure: legitimate pleasure and illegitimate pleasure. Legitimate pleasure is something you pay for in advance and then enjoy. Illegitimate pleasure is something you enjoy before you pay for it. After the interest is accrued, you end up paying much more for it in the end.

Here is an example: If a person starts a business by taking advantage of poor people or using illegal resources, it is illegitimate in the spirit. God blesses hard work, and if you are obedient to Him, You will eat of the good of the land.

Work hard and stay in the land of integrity, and God will bless your generations. Faith without works is dead. When you walk in integrity, God takes pleasure in blessing you.

Give that pleasure back to Him and bless the Lord. *Selah!*

Today declare…

> *The work of my hands is blessed by the Lord. I operate with willingness, obedience, and integrity. I shall eat the good of the land.*

THE POWER TO WALK IN LOVE

When the day of Pentecost had come, they were all together in one place. Suddenly a sound like a mighty rushing wind came from heaven, and ... they were all filled with the Holy Spirit and began to speak in other tongues, as the Spirit enabled them to speak.

—Acts 2:1–4

O n the Day of Pentecost the Holy Spirit broke through the atmosphere and filled people with God's power. Not just the power to cast out devils and speak in tongues but also the power to *love*. This is how you can identify true believers. They have the power to love, and because they have the power to love they can speak the truth in love and stand for what is right.

If you are not filled with the Holy Spirit, ask the Lord to fill you now with the evidence of speaking in other tongues. And if you have already been filled with the Spirit, ask for a fresh infilling. When you experience the power of Pentecost, out of your belly shall flow rivers of living water. And you will receive power to walk in love. *Selah!*

Today declare...

> *I receive a fresh infilling of the Holy Spirit. Through His power, I speak the truth in love and stand for what is right. I am overflowing with living water.*

_____

_____

_____

_____

_____

_____

_____

_____

_____

_____

_____

_____

_____

_____

_____

_____

_____

_____

_____

_____

_____

_____

_____

TASTE AND SEE

Oh, taste and see that the Lord is good.
—Psalm 34:8

❧

THE BIBLE SAYS to taste and see that the Lord is good. This means we can experience God with our senses. We can:

+ Taste Him (Ps. 34:8)
+ Feel Him (Acts 17:27)
+ See (or know) Him (Eph. 1:17)
+ Hear Him (John 10:5)
+ Smell Him (Exod. 40:5)

The opposite of "taste and see" is to "see and not taste." This is a curse, and in my opinion, the worst curse you can experience. It is like having a cake you cannot eat. The world says you can't have your cake and eat it too. This is a lie from the pit. What is the purpose of having a cake you cannot eat? There is none!

Second Kings 7:2 tells of an officer the king relied on as his right-hand man. The prophet Elisha prophesied prosperity in a time of famine. But the officer negated the word of the prophet, and because of his unbelief Elisha proclaimed that the officer would *see* the prophecy fulfilled but not *taste* it. What a curse to have your promise manifest but not be able to enjoy it!

The Holy Spirit is not some "thing." He is not a figure of someone's imagination or a character in a fable. He is a part of the Godhead who lives inside us. He is to be experienced. You can sense Him. I challenge you to taste of (experience) the Holy Spirit. He wants to fill every empty place in your life. *Selah.*

Today declare...

> *I will taste and see the goodness and power of the Holy Spirit. Every empty place in my life will be filled with His presence.*

_____

_____

_____

_____

_____

_____

_____

_____

_____

_____

_____

_____

_____

_____

A THOUSAND GENERATIONS
OF BLESSINGS

*Know therefore that the LORD your God, He is God, the faithful
God, who keeps covenant and mercy with them who love Him
and keep His commandments to a thousand generations.*
—DEUTERONOMY 7:9

PEOPLE OFTEN SPEAK of my past, and that is OK. The devil is defeated by my testimony. I declare that eyes have not seen and ears have not heard, neither has it entered in the mind of man what God has in store for me and my seed! Instead of a generational curse, my seed will reap a thousand generations of blessings. My children are the heritage of the Lord, and the fruit of my womb is blessed because they are a reward from the Lord. He knew them before they were even formed in my womb.

Speak life over your seed. Confess what God says over them because if you don't, what the devil is saying will have room to manifest. Give no room to the enemy.

When I took my twin boys to college, I prayed that God would send His destiny angel before them and that the flavor of favor would be their portion. I bound all accidents, incidents, and injuries in Jesus's name, and I prayed that the Holy Ghost would put fire on their feet and give them a trailblazing anointing to make a path for our future generations.

Do the same for your children. Decree things and speak things that are not as though they were over your seed. *Selah!*

Today declare...

> *My seed will reap a thousand generations of blessings. Eyes have not seen nor have ears heard, neither has it entered in their minds what God has for them. My children are the heritage of the Lord. The fruit of my womb is blessed. May the flavor of favor be their portion.*

_____

_____

_____

_____

_____

_____

_____

_____

_____

_____

_____

_____

_____

_____

THE PEACE OF GOD

*And the peace of God, which surpasses all understanding, will
protect your hearts and minds through Christ Jesus.*
—PHILIPPIANS 4:7

JOHN 14:27 SAYS that Jesus gives us His peace. This peace
cannot come from the world. Because of this peace, we
should not be troubled or fearful in our minds about the
cares of this world.

A lot of people have no peace because they have no patience.
The Word says to be anxious for nothing, but by prayer and
supplication with thanksgiving, to let your requests be made
known unto God (Phil. 4:6). Only then will a peace that surpasses all human understanding be your portion. This peace
will guard your heart and mind, and the foolishness that the
devil wants to distract you with will have no teeth.

Then, as Romans 16:20 states, the God of peace will soon
crush Satan under your feet, but you must wait on God.
Peace gives you the ability to wait!

Joy and faith are twins. Romans 15:13 says, "May the God
of hope fill you with all joy and peace in believing, so that
you may abound in hope, through the power of the Holy
Spirit." To set your mind on the flesh is death, but to set
your mind on the Spirit is life and *peace.*

Today declare...

> *My mind is set on the Spirit of God, who is life
> and peace.*

_____

_____

_____

_____

_____

_____

_____

_____

_____

_____

_____

_____

_____

_____

_____

_____

_____

_____

PEACE BE STILL!

He rose and rebuked the wind, and said to the sea, "Peace, be
still!" Then the wind ceased and there was a great calm.

—MARK 4:39

I HEAR FROM MANY people who feel they are under attack
and have no hope. If that describes you, I prophesy peace
to your natural mind and to the spirit of your mind. Do not
give people a "piece" of your mind because it will make peace
leave your mind. I speak to every storm that rages in your
life: *"Peace be still!"*

To practice peace, you must give up hate. A hater cannot
have peace. Let the love of God cover your mind so that
revenge and retaliation do not consume you and hinder your
blessings. Jesus loves you. Have peace and rest in that. *Selah.*

Today declare . . .

> *The love of God covers my mind. Revenge and*
> *retaliation will not consume me. There is great*
> *calm in my life, and the blessings of God flow freely.*

_____

_____

_____

_____

_____

_____

_____

_____

_____

_____

_____

_____

_____

_____

_____

_____

_____

_____

_____

_____

_____

_____

_____

_____

_____

_____

_____

_____

_____

BELIEVE, BREATHE, RECEIVE, AND BE RELIEVED

Finally, brothers, whatever things are true, whatever things are honest, whatever things are just, whatever things are pure, whatever things are lovely, whatever things are of good report, if there is any virtue, and if there is any praise, think on these things.

—PHILIPPIANS 4:8

THIS IS THE season to believe, breathe, receive, and be relieved (BBRR). So many people are bound by stress. They have high blood pressure and all kinds of stress-related physical problems. That is not what God wants for us.

When I go to the doctor and he gives me a negative blood-pressure report, I ask him to give me five minutes. I cut the lights off, take a deep breath, relax, and think on Philippians 4:8:

> Finally, brothers, whatever things are true, whatever things are honest, whatever things are just, whatever things are pure, whatever things are lovely, whatever things are of good report, if there is any virtue, and if there is any praise, think on these things.

In other words, that verse is saying not to let lies; what is dishonest, unfair, or unclean; or ugly negative reports that have no power and do not give God praise crowd your mind.

When I close my eyes and meditate on what I should be thinking of, forsaking what was troubling me before I went into the doctor's office, my blood-pressure reading is perfect! Our minds send messages to our bodies, and our bodies respond accordingly.

What messages have you been sending to your body? I plead the blood of Jesus over your mind, will, intellect, and emotions. I command your mind to be cleansed of all impure thoughts. I decree that the healing Balm of Gilead and the same virtue that flowed through Jesus's garment will flow through your brain waves to every part of your body.

BBRR—believe, breathe, receive, and be relieved. Before you can be released into a new thing, sometimes you have to get relief from the things weighing you down. Take a deep breath and live. You have only one life, and it is worth living. *Selah.*

Today pray...

> *Lord, I plead the blood of Jesus over my mind, will, intellect, and emotions. In Your Son's name, I command my mind to be cleansed of all impure thoughts. I decree that the healing Balm of Gilead and the same virtue that flowed through Jesus's garment will flow through my brain waves and into every part of my body. In Jesus's name, amen.*

_____

_____

_____

_____

_____

_____

IT'S TIME TO GET REAL

*...that He might present to Himself a glorious church,
not having spot, or wrinkle, or any such thing, but
that it should be holy and without blemish.*

—Ephesians 5:27

I preached a sermon at a service for the ladies at church titled "Hiding Behind the Lipstick." It was one of the most anointed meetings I've attended in a while. Ladies gave testimonies of how they hid behind things in their lives while they kept smiles on their pretty faces. There was deliverance, healing, and most of all, fellowship. Everybody focused on what God needed to do in their lives.

The Bible mentions the rulers of the darkness of this world (Eph. 6:12). The Greek word translated "rulers" is *kosmokratōr*. It describes someone who cosmetically fixes things up in the world to look pretty when they are really ugly. Makeup covers the blemishes, but God is coming back for a church without spot, wrinkle, or blemish.

Let's not fake it till we make it. Jesus is real, and we need to get real. No more hiding behind the lipstick. *Selah.*

Today declare...

> *I will not hide behind cover-ups, cosmetic fixes, or fake smiles. I will be real with Jesus because He is real with me.*

DO NOT PLAY WITH DARKNESS!

For even Satan disguises himself as an angel of light.
—2 CORINTHIANS 11:14

WHEN I WAS a little girl, my sisters and I used to get in front of the mirror and call on Bloody Mary. Thank God, she never came! As teenagers, my friends used to play with the Ouija board, but I was too scared to participate. I never told anyone, but I used to be afraid of the dark. Today I am not afraid of the dark, but I do not play with darkness.

A Greek word for darkness used in the Bible is *skotos*. Another is *skotia*. These words relate to things that are unclear and obscure. The worst kind of bondage is not when things are totally black but actually when they are gray. This kind of darkness is not so obvious. The devil comes as an angel of light. Because he is the prince of darkness and comes in a fake light, the manifestation is a demonic dirty gray. Even God says it is worse to be lukewarm than to be either hot or cold; it is better to be either in the church or in the world than on the fence.

I said all that to say this: as we get closer to the return of Jesus, things will get not blacker but grayer. Deception is the greatest power of the enemy. The supernatural operates from both sides, darkness and light. Most people do not willingly operate in darkness, so the enemy presents a gray area that seems acceptable.

An Internet craze among youth today is to summon a demon named Charlie. It is similar to the Bloody Mary or other paranormal games. These games are not harmless. The truth is that children are dabbling in the occult. The word *occult* means "secret." These occult spirits get stronger as they secretly hide behind the doors of witchcraft.

Not long ago a fifteen-year-old in Atlanta died while conjuring the presence of Charlie in the name of having fun. The young lady was diagnosed as having a heart attack. Sadly, she died a horrible death in front of two of her friends.[1]

Charlie is said to be an ancient Mexican spirit called upon as the participants put two pencils in the shape of a cross and dare the demon to come out. As these children discovered, there is nothing fun about playing with darkness. It brings serious consequences. Even today Satan comes to steal, kill, and destroy. Know what your children are doing online. Don't let them dabble with darkness—and don't play with it yourself either. Walk in the light. *Selah.*

Today pray…

> *Father, in the name of Jesus, I bind the spirit of Charlie and all other demons coming through the spirit of deception, especially to our youth. Let them be secure in their knowledge of who You are, in Jesus's name. Amen.*

———————————————————————————

———————————————————————————

———————————————————————————

———————————————————————————

———————————————————————————

———————————————————————————

WALK WORTHY OF
YOUR CALLING

*I, therefore, the prisoner of the Lord, exhort you to walk in a
manner worthy of the calling with which you were called.*

—EPHESIANS 4:1

PSALM 75:6–7 HAS been a safety net for me over the years.
I believe it is a foundational key for success. It basically
says that promotion does not come from the east, west, or
south. It comes from the north—the secret place in God.

You cannot fail when you stay within the perimeter of
your calling or occupation. The Bible says to "walk worthy of
the vocation wherewith ye are called" (Eph. 4:1, KJV). Truly,
I am called to write. Am I the best writer? No! But I'm called
to do it. I am the best at writing Kimberly Daniels's books!
Nobody can write my books better than I can. I have written
sixteen books and sold over half a million copies. Go, Jesus!

There is a difference between liking to write, wanting
to write, and being called to write. Just because you teach
English does not mean you are called to be a columnist. Just
because you are a preacher does not mean you are called to
write books. Writing is an anointing. It's called "the anointing
of the scribe." It's something you are born to do. Yes, we need
training and education, but that cannot be our God. Intellect
and natural power cannot be our sources of confidence.

Promotion comes from God. He opens doors, but He
uses people to turn the knob for you to get you in that door.

John Eckhardt, the late C. Peter Wagner, and *Charisma* magazine turned the knob for me.

Be careful of covetousness and false ambition. Don't waste your precious days on Earth trying to do something someone else is called to do. Walk worthy of *your* vocation, and you will always be successful.

Walking in someone else's steps may trip you, and trying to wear their shoes could make you fall. Be careful of the Peter Principle: being promoted to failure. This is how the enemy sets us up. He can open a door that you are not qualified to walk in, and when that happens, you will be left unequipped and unsure.

Writing is not just a skill; it is a gift from God. It comes not from the head but from the heart. I hear from many people who want to pursue their callings to write. I pray the spirit of the scribe to your heart. I release uncommon favor to your life. Whatever you are called to do, walk in it. Promotion comes from God. *Selah.*

Today declare…

> *I will walk worthy of my calling. I will not walk in someone else's assignment. What God has for me is for me, and I receive His promotion in His time.*

_____

_____

_____

_____

_____

_____

BINDING AZAZEL: THE DEMON OF TRANSFER

The goat on which the lot falls to be the scapegoat shall be presented
alive before the LORD to make atonement with it, that it may be
sent away as a scapegoat into the wilderness . . . And Aaron shall lay
both his hands on the head of the live goat, and confess over it all
the iniquities of the children of Israel, and all their transgressions
in all their sins, putting them on the head of the goat, and shall
send it away by the hand of a designated man into the wilderness.

—LEVITICUS 16:10, 21

A HORROR MOVIE RELEASED last year stars the demon "Charlie." When the movie *The Gallows* was about to come out, I urged people not to see it and not to let their children see it. As I mentioned before, a teenage girl in Atlanta died while summoning this demon in a game called the Charlie Challenge.[1] When playing this game, kids will put pencils in the form of a cross over a piece of paper with the words *yes* and *no* written on it. They will then attempt to summon the demon by saying, "Charlie, Charlie, are you here?" The spirit will move the pencil to either yes or no.

The fifteen-year-old and her friends probably didn't realize it at the time, but demons are real. Thank God that Jesus is more real!

The enemy uses games like the Charlie Challenge and movies like *The Gallows* to influence people. Bind Azazel, the demon of transfer, the scapegoat mentioned in Leviticus 16. This is how spirits transfer.

I declare that the gates of hell shall not prevail against the church. Let every demonic gateway to this generation be closed and locked up forever. Let demon spirits masquerading as harmless "Charlie" be exposed and the children of believers and nonbelievers be protected from their power. I plead the blood of Jesus over our children! *Selah.*

Today pray...

> *Father God, in the name of Jesus, I pray that every portal Charlie would travel through to get into the lives of my children be shut. I declare that the gates of hell shall not prevail against the church. Let every gateway from Charlie to this generation be closed and locked up forever. Let Charlie be exposed and the children in my sphere of influence be protected from his power. In Jesus's name, amen.*

_____

_____

_____

_____

_____

_____

_____

_____

THE SILVER LINING

*When I form a cloud over the Earth and the rainbow appears in
the cloud, I'll remember my covenant between me and you.*
—GENESIS 9:13, THE MESSAGE

ONE DAY A CLOUD with a silver lining got my attention.
The silver lining was so beautiful that I took a picture of
it, but the shadow behind the cloud was thought-provoking.

A shadow is produced by a body that comes between a ray
of light and a surface. There was a ray of light behind this
cloud, but the shadow was against the sky. When I magnified
the picture of the cloud, I noticed a rainbow behind it filled
with beautiful colors.

The rainbow represents the promise God made to His
people. Anything else said about the rainbow is of the flesh.
Only God can make a rainbow as a reminder that He keeps
His promises to His people. And not only does He keep His
promises—He *is* the promise!

+ Hosea 14:7 says those who live in God's shadow
  will return and flourish like the grain.

+ Psalm 91:1 says he who dwells in the shelter of
  the Most High will abide in the shadow of the
  Almighty.

+ Psalm 57:1 says we can hide in the shadow of His
  wings until destruction passes by.

- Psalm 63:7 says we can rejoice in the shadow of His wings because He has been our help.

- Psalm 121:5 says the Lord is our keeper, and He is the shade on our right hand.

- Isaiah 4:5–6 says "the LORD will create over the whole area of Mount Zion and over her assemblies a cloud by day, even smoke, and the brightness of a flaming fire by night; for over all the glory will be a canopy. There will be a shelter to give shade from the heat by day, and refuge and protection from the storm and the rain" (NASB).

Whose shadow is that behind the cloud in your life? *Selah.* Pause and think on that!

Today pray...

> *Thank You, God, for remembering Your promises to me. Thank You for being the faithful One. I pray that with every dark cloud, I will recognize You as the silver lining. You are my shelter and shadow, protecting and shielding me from destruction. You are my keeper, and I praise You. Amen.*

_____

_____

_____

_____

_____

_____

EVERY GOOD AND PERFECT GIFT

*Every good gift and every perfect gift is from above and comes down
from the Father of lights, with whom is no change or shadow of turning.*

—JAMES 1:17

❧

M Y YOUNGEST BOYS are now in college. It seems as if
it were only yesterday that I gave birth to the twins,
Elijah and Elisha, and now they're big, strong men.

It was exciting to get them ready to leave for the University
of Maryland, where they have full football scholarships. It is a
blessing that they will not only get a quality education but also
be able to operate in the gift God gave them—playing football!

Many attempt to downplay young men who earn athletic
scholarships, believing it is more prestigious to go to
Harvard or Yale to become an attorney. Not so in my book!
James 1:17 says every good and perfect gift comes from God.
Though my boys are academically smart, they stand out on
the football field.

We all receive our lot in life. Only *God* could cause two
boys who came from the same womb at the same time to
become two of the top fifty defensive backs in the United
States and then send them to an NCAA Division I university.
Go, Jesus! What are the chances of that happening? That's
nothing but the goodness of God.

Depending on their intellect, bloodline, or wealth may
work for some people, but I give God all the credit for the
successes in my life and in my children's lives. Yes, the boys
still have to walk the road ahead of them, but the destiny

angel has already gone down that road to pave the way. God has done the same for you. He has prepared the way for you to complete the assignment He has given you.

Take authority over every spirit that is lying in wait to trip you up as you travel down the road God has mapped out for you. That's what I've done for my boys. I've taken authority over every spirit that has been put in place to keep black male athletes from fulfilling their destinies in God, and I've dealt with every generational curse through my repentance.

If you haven't already done so, break any generational curse that may be operating in your life by repenting of every sin that would keep you or your children from fulfilling their destinies. You can pray:

> *Lord, forgive me of all my sins, whether committed knowingly or unknowingly, that have come through thoughts, words, or acts so that I (and my children) will be free from generational contamination. Lord, I praise You for the victory.*

Then choose to walk in righteousness and obedience to God and His Word. That will not only keep the chains of bondage broken but also establish a new legacy for future generations.

Don't leave your future to chance. God hasn't. Every good and perfect gift comes from Him, and if you choose to follow His path, He will lead you straight into your destiny.

Today pray …

> *Lord, I thank You that every good and perfect gift comes from You. I am not blessed because of my own strengths and abilities but because of Your favor. I declare that all Your plans for my life will*

be accomplished. I take authority over every spirit
that would seek to trip me up as I walk along the
path to my destiny. Send your destiny angel to pave
the way. I decree that the centrifugal forces of God
will flow through my feet and all of creation will
line up with my purpose. In Jesus's name. Amen.

_____

_____

_____

_____

_____

_____

_____

_____

_____

_____

_____

_____

_____

_____

_____

REBUILDING THE WALLS

Finally, I said to them, "You see the distress that we are in, how Jerusalem is devastated and its gates are burned with fire. Come, and let us rebuild the wall of Jerusalem so that we will no more be a reproach."

—NEHEMIAH 2:17

WEAPONS WILL FORM, but God promises that they will not prosper. During Nehemiah's time, the enemy devastated the walls of Jerusalem. The same thing seems to be happening today, as many of the cities in America are under siege. Nehemiah, whom I consider the greatest leader of all time, understood that to rebuild the walls of his city three things needed attention:

1. The walls
2. The gates
3. The rubbish

To protect the walls, there were watchmen posted high up on the walls to see attacks from afar. Their assignment was to warn the city of attacks by sounding the alarm. Spiritual watchmen do the same; they sound the alarm of enemy attacks.

At the gates were gatekeepers who controlled the traffic of the city, determining what came in and out. In the spiritual realm spiritual gatekeepers determine what is forbidden and what is allowed through binding and loosing.

They make decrees and declarations to establish the vision of the city.

The rubbish reflects the negative influence destruction and infiltration have on a city after an attack. Rubbish such as gossip, backbiting, divisiveness, and doubt infiltrate the hearts and minds of the people. The only way to get rid of rubbish like this is to stand in the gaps of the city streets. The Spirit of the Lord searches for and anoints individuals to do so.

Are you an intercessor for your city? Are you a watchman or a gatekeeper? Do the walls of your city need to be rebuilt? Are you paying attention to the walls, the gates, and the gaps of your city? Do you sense a need to deal with the rubbish that is infiltrating our ministries?

The answer to the demonic siege on our cities is for Christians to pray. Let's build a prayer wall around the churches of America. Our religious liberty is under attack every day because the enemy wants to silence us. To rebuild the walls in your city through prayer:

1. List the major prayer concerns in your city.

2. Under each concern list decrees and declarations with scriptures to support them and target those concerns in prayer.

3. Get at least twelve leaders to agree to be a part of the prayer effort for your city with you.

4. Have people praying, whether together or separate, at appointed times each day. And then watch God!

Let's take our cities back for Jesus! Let's get rid of the rubbish to rebuild the wall. *Selah*.

Today pray...

> *Lord, I stand in the gap for my city. I pray that You will send intercessors and watchmen to repair the walls and gates of the city and to remove the rubbish. In Jesus's name, amen.*

_____

_____

_____

_____

_____

_____

_____

_____

_____

_____

_____

_____

_____

_____

_____

_____

_____

ALLOW GOD TO REDIRECT YOU

In all your ways acknowledge Him, and He will direct your paths.
—PROVERBS 3:6

GOD IS SMARTER than we are. That's why you should thank God that your steps are ordered *by Him*! Allow God to direct and redirect you on life's path; He can see far beyond where you want to go.

Recently while in prayer I saw an angel of the Lord with a sword drawn. A person was riding a donkey, trying to move down a path the angel was blocking (with his sword drawn). The donkey kept bucking and would not move forward, just as in the story about Balaam's donkey in Numbers 22:23. The donkey could see the trouble ahead, but the person riding it could not. Eventually God opened the eyes of the rider so he could see the angel with the sword drawn.

God orders our steps. He is omniscient, and He sees all. When we're going in a direction and extreme turbulence is manifesting in our circumstances, we may need to consider our way. It is prideful to attempt to force something that simply does not fit. There is a way that seems right to a man, but the end of that way is death (Prov. 14:12).

Never be afraid to turn around or start over. Do not endure illegitimate warfare. There is no victory in fighting a battle you're not called to face. Turning around is not giving up but shifting. If you're relying on God to direct your steps, let Him shift you. It may save your life. I thank God for saving my life so many times!

Father, open our spiritual eyes. *Selah.*

Today pray...

> *Lord, I surrender to You. You see far ahead and far beyond what I can see. I invite You to come into my life and redirect me so that I will be in step with You. Order my steps, God. Shift me. Lead me in the way I should go. In Jesus's name, I pray. Amen.*

_____

_____

_____

_____

_____

_____

_____

_____

_____

_____

_____

_____

_____

SO BLESSED YOU DON'T KNOW HOW TO ACT

Things are going to happen so fast your head will swim, one thing fast on the heels of the other. You won't be able to keep up. Everything will be happening at once—and everywhere you look, blessings! Blessings like wine pouring off the mountains and hills.

—AMOS 9:13–14, THE MESSAGE

SOMETIMES GOD BLESSES you so good that you don't know how to act. Don't ever get so used to the blessings that you can't give God the response He wants from you. Forget what people think and enjoy the special moments of blessing God gives you in life.

When God blesses you, don't act as if you've never been through anything. If you've ever been through something, when God blesses you, you automatically give Him the response He wants, which is to praise Him. Have you ever given someone a gift and the person acted as if he could take it or leave it? Don't do that to God. He's been too good to us for us not to praise Him.

Some people receive blessings and still act ugly because they have holes in their souls. They are never content. No matter what God does, they always look for something else. They even covet others' blessings. They don't realize that their attitude is limiting what God can do in their lives.

Guess what? God has a tailor-made blessing for you! But don't live your life praying for God to bless only you. Walk in thanksgiving and clear your personal prayer list so you can stand in the gap for someone else.

People of God, we need to be more than saved and sanctified. We need to be satisfied. God will do exceedingly and abundantly above all we can ask or even imagine. And when He does, we need to act as if He has blessed us! *Selah.*

Today pray...

> *Lord, I receive Your tailor-made blessings for me. Bless me so good that I won't know how to act. Let me never get used to how You bless me. I will be careful to give You all the praise and glory. In Jesus's name, amen.*

_____

_____

_____

_____

_____

_____

_____

_____

_____

_____

_____

THE BLESSING IN SEEING
THE PROMISE FULFILLED

*I will open my mouth in a parable; I will utter insightful sayings
of old, which we have heard and known, what our fathers
have told us. We will not hide them from their children, but
will tell the coming generation the praises of the LORD, and
His strength, and the wonderful works that He has done.*

—PSALM 78:2–4

GOD PROMISED ABRAHAM that his seed would be as great as the number of stars in the sky, as far as he could see. Young people need to *see* examples of other young people who have manifested fulfilled promises in their lives. They need to *see* young people with success stories, people who can handle the blessing of God and not forget Him.

I prophesy that our children will do great exploits and not forget God in the process. They need to *see* what is possible when a young person chooses to live for God. Tomorrow is promised to no one, not even to our youth. One of the twins' teammates went to sleep one night and did not wake up the next morning. He died in his sleep. My sister told me of another young man, a former student of hers, who had lost his mind and was eating from the trash.

We need to pray for our children's destinies! We need to cover them in prayer and tell them about Jesus now, whether the world likes it or not. Jesus is coming back soon. We must watch as well as pray. *Selah!*

Today declare...

> *My children will do great exploits because they have witnessed the faithfulness of God. They will not forget the God of their youth. I speak blessing and favor over their destinies.*

_____

_____

_____

_____

_____

_____

_____

_____

_____

_____

_____

_____

_____

_____

_____

_____

_____

_____

EXPECT TO BE BLESSED

And all these blessings will come on you and overtake you
if you listen to the voice of the LORD your God.
—DEUTERONOMY 28:2

FEAR IS A spirit, and the greatest fear is the fear of tomorrow. Today is the day that the Lord has made and we should rejoice in it; we should have no thought (or fear) for tomorrow. Displace the spirit of fear with the anointing of expectation.

The enemy always wants us to expect the worst. But God says, "I know the thoughts that I think toward you, saith the LORD, thoughts of peace, and not of evil, to give you an expected end" (Jer. 29:11, KJV). In other words, God wants to give us hope in the final outcome of whatever we are facing. The word translated "expected" in Jeremiah 29:11 is *tiqvah* in Hebrew. It is like a cord that connects us to the thing that we expect or long for.

Instead of fearing tomorrow, expect the blessings of the Lord to manifest in your life. Expect God to expose and blot out your enemies. Expect Him to set you free from all bondages. Expect God to bring you into your promised land, your place of destiny, and for the enemy to restore sevenfold everything he has stolen from you (Prov. 6:31). Rest in the Lord and expect the blessings of the Lord to come upon you and overtake you. *Selah!*

Today pray...

> *Lord, I displace the spirit of fear with the anointing of expectation. I expect Your best and not the worst. May all my enemies be exposed and expelled, and may I be liberated and set free from all bondages. May all that is owed to me be returned in the name of Jesus. May a spirit of rest come upon me in this season, in Jesus's name. Amen.*

WHEN WOMEN COME TOGETHER

*In those days Mary arose and quickly went into the hill country,
to a city of Judah, and entered the house of Zechariah and
greeted Elizabeth. When Elizabeth heard the greeting of Mary,
the baby leaped in her womb. And Elizabeth was filled with
the Holy Spirit. She spoke out with a loud voice, "Blessed are
you among women, and blessed is the fruit of your womb!"*

—LUKE 1:39–42

IT'S CRAZY WHEN God pours His blessings on you and
people become jealous. It almost makes you scared to
testify. This is a major problem among women.

The devil understands that if we touch and agree and celebrate every sister's blessings, all hell will have to back up. After
the fall of mankind, God put enmity between the serpent
and the fruit of the woman's womb. (I call women "men with
wombs"!) The word translated "enmity" is *ebah* in the Hebrew;
it means a deep-seated hatred for the devil. The trick of the
enemy is to make us use this enmity against one another.

God put this enmity in us to bust devils, not each other!
Let's vow not to hate but to celebrate one another as women.
The worst words to release when someone gets blessed are,
"When am I gonna get mine?" or, "What about me, Lord?" A
jealous spirit gets quiet when someone shares her good news.

I believe the Lord showed me that this is the blocker of
many blessings. Let's renounce this blocking spirit and prepare our hearts for a new season. I believe revival is coming
to the "men with wombs." It's time for us to be like Elizabeth

and Mary, touching and agreeing until our babies jump in our wombs. Mary didn't get jealous because Elizabeth had John the Baptist in her womb. And Elizabeth didn't get jealous that Mary was carrying Jesus in hers.

Preachers like Medina Pullings and Cindy Trimm make my "baby" jump. When we have ministered together, the anointing to "put some things to flight" was clearly present. We should not *compete with* one another but *complete* one another. Fitly joined when we come together, we each bring what is needed to serve God's overall purpose.

God has given us power—*exousia* (individual, dedicated special ability)—over all the power of the enemy. Come on, ladies. I'm ready to connect my *exousia* to that of other ladies ministering the gospel so together we can do the greater works Jesus spoke of. *Selah.*

Today declare…

> *May all hell back up as I stand with my sisters in Christ, celebrating their blessings. I renounce any blocking spirit operating in me against other women. I vow not to hate but to celebrate what God is doing in and through women's lives.*

_____

_____

_____

_____

_____

_____

MORE VALUABLE THAN RUBIES

Who can find a virtuous woman? For her worth is far above rubies.
—PROVERBS 31:10

༄

I HAVE A FRIEND who told me a story about a ring. She and her husband were shopping at a garage sale and they saw a ring in a decorative box. They showed the owner of the house the ring, and he said it was just a gaudy old ring and was not worth much. He told my friend and her husband they could have it for fifty cents.

My friend bought the ring for half a dollar and took it home. As she examined it carefully, she noticed some writing inside the ring and asked her husband about it. He said the writing was the European inscription for eighteen carats. They thought, "If the ring is eighteen carats, then the diamonds may be legitimate." When they took the ring to an appraiser, they found out the diamonds were special-cut and the ring was very valuable. And they paid only fifty cents!

This story reminded me of relationships. Some people cannot discern the value of people God has placed in their lives. Because of a familiar spirit, they can't see the worth of the person they have become so comfortable with. They say, "Oh, that thing has been around here for a while—it's not worth anything!" As a result, they give it away.

But when the right person takes a closer look, the true worth is revealed! Remember, one person's trash is another's treasure. Be careful what you throw away or even give away. It may be difficult to get again. And you will spend the rest of your life seeking what you can never find. Appreciation adds value to anything! *Selah.*

Today declare...

> *I value and appreciate the relationships God has placed in my life. Their worth is far above rubies.*

_____

_____

_____

_____

_____

_____

_____

_____

_____

_____

_____

_____

_____

_____

_____

_____

_____

YOU ARE GOING IN THIS TIME

A thousand may fall at your side and ten thousand at your right hand,
but it shall not come near you. Only with your eyes shall you behold
and see the reward of the wicked. Because you have made the LORD,
who is my refuge, even the Most High, your dwelling, there shall be
no evil befall you, neither shall any plague come near your tent.

—PSALM 91:7–10

A THOUSAND MAY FALL to one side, ten thousand to the other, but no harm will come nigh your dwelling. Keep your eyes on Jesus, who is the author and the finisher of your faith. While you're running this race, many will try to trip you. But continue to keep your eyes on the finish line. I break the curse of almost, not enough, and barely making it. You will not sit outside the promised land plagued by what could have been. You are going in this time!

The spirit of limbo is not your portion. You are not between blessings. You are smack-dab in the middle of the will of God. Don't be afraid of your accusers. Esther made sure Haman, the man trying to kill her people, came to her banquet. Lift your head up. God is about to deliver you from your persecutors—but first He is preparing a table for you in the presence of your enemies. It's a big table because there are giants in the land.

Hear the word of the Lord: *you are well able!* You and your children will eat of the good of the land. Don't give up. You are down the street from destiny. Move forward and don't look back! *Selah.*

Today declare...

> *The curse of "almost," "not enough," and "barely making it" is broken over my life, in the name of Jesus. I will not sit outside the promised land. I will go in!*

_____

_____

_____

_____

_____

_____

_____

_____

_____

_____

_____

_____

_____

_____

_____

GET READY FOR A SEVENFOLD RETURN!

*But if [the thief] is found, he will restore sevenfold;
he will give all the substance of his house.*

—PROVERBS 6:31

THERE HAVE BEEN seventy Jubilees since the walls of Jericho came down. Ever since that seventieth Jubilee in September 2015, I have been encouraging people to remember:

1. The anointing is coming on the next generation as never before, so keep speaking into the ears of Joshua (the next generation).

2. The walls of Jericho did not come down for nothing. God gave the people of Israel the land promised to them. This means that their enemies were openly defeated. This is a time of restoration. God is about to disgrace the thing that tried to keep you away from your promise. (Go ahead and shout now! Praise Him in advance.)

3. During a Jubilee the land has to go back to its original owner. I believe that in the aftermath of the seventieth Jubilee, we can expect not only that God will bless us with whatever we're believing Him for but also that

everything that was originally ours and was taken is going to be returned. Proverbs 6:31 says that when you recognize a thief, he *must* return what he stole seven times. You'd better recognize!

Holla! Now would be a good time to shout. The walls are coming down! *Selah.*

Today declare . . .

> *The walls that are keeping me from my blessing are coming down. I receive sevenfold restoration for all the enemy has stolen from me.*

_____

_____

_____

_____

_____

_____

_____

_____

_____

_____

_____

GOD IS A MIRACLE-WORKER

*Jesus went throughout all the cities and villages, teaching in
their synagogues, preaching the gospel of the kingdom, and
healing every sickness and every disease among the people.*

—MATTHEW 9:35

GOD IS STILL in the miracle-working business, whether
you believe it or not!

A few years ago I landed back in my city after traveling.
I had only a few minutes before our church service started,
and since I had scheduled another speaker, I went home
because I didn't think I could make it to church before the
service began. I threw on a raggedy T-shirt and some long
shorts and flip-flops and started doing some cleaning.

As I was sweeping the floor, the Lord said, "Go to church
and preach—now!" Questioning God in my mind, I thought,
"Surely the speaker is already up. It's too late. I'm not dressed."
But I called and told the elders I was on my way to preach. I
didn't even change clothes because God demanded that I go
as I was. He instructed me to talk about the supernatural
things I had experienced over the years. Wearing flip-flops,
a T-shirt, and long shorts, I testified—and I was on fire! I
declared that every person would be healed *that night*!

I did not know a boy was in the back of the church in a
wheelchair. As they rolled him to the front, I actually thought,
"Uh oh!" This young man had not eaten or spoken in months.
His body was so twisted that he looked inches shorter. But
when I laid hands on him, I heard his bones cracking. God

was straightening his body before my very eyes. I said out loud, "Well, go ahead and get out of that wheelchair!" And he did "with quickness," like he was never in a wheelchair.

After he walked, he said, "I'm hungry and want to go to Burger King." I know those words were like music to his mother's ears since he hadn't spoken in so long. This boy had been carried up the steps of the church in a wheelchair, but when he left he was practically running to Burger King after having had no appetite for months.

God gave this young man a miracle! When he came to church that day, he did not believe in ministries that cast out devils and prayed for people to get up out of wheelchairs. But God made a believer out of him. That young man visited Spoken Word again recently, and seeing him made me want to remind you that God is no respecter of persons. He is still in the miracle-working business!

Today pray . . .

> *God, I believe You are still in the miracle-working business. I decree that You will restore health to me and heal me of every wound (Jer. 30:17). And when others see the miracle, You will make believers out of them, in Jesus's name. Amen.*

_____

_____

_____

_____

_____

TO THE LEAST OF THESE

*"For I was hungry and you gave Me food, I was thirsty and
you gave Me drink, I was a stranger and you took Me in. I
was naked and you clothed Me, I was sick and you visited
Me, I was in prison and you came to Me."... The King will
answer, "Truly I say to you, as you have done it for one of the
least of these brothers of Mine, you have done it for Me."*

—MATTHEW 25:35–36, 40

I WAS WALKING INTO a store one night and saw a man
outside begging. I was in a rush, and I know much of the
time beggars are people running a scam, so I immediately
blew this man off.

But I noticed that the man's pants were unzipped, and as
I looked up to tell him to zip his pants, I could see from his
eyes that he was not there. (Matthew 6:22 tells us the eye is
the lamp of the body.) His mind had been taken captive.

Sounding like a child learning how to talk, the man said,
"I hungry!" My heart fell to my stomach. Immediately I took
him in the store and bought him some food.

That experience reminded me that not every beggar is
running a game. Jesus said when we minister to the "least of
these," we minister to Him. You never know. You could be
entertaining angels unaware (Heb. 13:2).

Pay attention to the eyes of the people you come in
contact with. When people can't look into your eyes, it's
often because they are afraid for you to see who they really
are. *Selah!*

Today pray...

Lord, increase my discernment to recognize the "least of these." Slow me down so that I can help the hungry, thirsty, stranger, naked, sick, and imprisoned. I know that when I minister to them, I am ministering to You. Thank You, Jesus, for opportunities to bless You. Amen.

_____

_____

_____

_____

_____

_____

_____

_____

_____

_____

_____

_____

_____

_____

IS THERE A JONAH
ON YOUR BOAT?

Then the men were very afraid and said to him, "What is this you have done?" For the men knew that he was fleeing from the presence of the LORD because he had told them....So Jonah said to them, "Pick me up and toss me into the sea. Then the sea will quiet down for you. For I know that it is on my account this great storm has come upon you."

—JONAH 1:10–12

BISHOP NOEL JONES spoke at a church in Jacksonville, Florida, recently, and he tore the house up. His message was tailor-made for everyone there. Putting it in a nutshell, he said if you are experiencing turmoil in your life, look around to see if you have a Jonah on your boat. You may be getting rid of stuff, trying to change things around you (in a panic) because the boat is about to sink, while Jonah is comfortably sleeping in the corner.

You will miss your moment with Jonah on your boat. No matter how good it looks, how much it cost, how bad it hurts, or what anyone thinks about it, get Jonah off the boat! *Selah.*

Today pray...

> *Lord, help me to see the Jonahs in my life, and give me the courage to get them off my boat. No Jonahs will cause me to miss my jubilee, in the name of Jesus. Amen.*

_____

_____

_____

_____

_____

_____

_____

_____

_____

_____

_____

_____

_____

_____

_____

_____

_____

_____

_____

_____

TWO THINGS ABOUT DOORS

He shall open, and no one shall shut. And he
shall shut, and no one shall open.

—ISAIAH 22:22

⁓✄⁓

GOD IS OPENING doors of opportunity for His people. He is canceling debts, bringing unexpected contracts, setting people free, putting houses in order, bringing members back into the church, restoring relationships, and giving His people rest. Praise the Lord!

When God spoke to me about bringing opportunity to His people, He also said to me, "In order for Me to loose you, I have to bind someone up. In order for Me to give you rest, I can allow your enemies no peace."

I see big doors in the spirit, but doors operate in two ways. Things come in, and things go out. Doors open and close. Be sensitive to the doors God wants to close. Closed doors are blessings too! God is closing doors behind you that you will not be able to go back into even if you try. By closing those doors, God is helping you to move forward—where the blessing is!

The draft of the closed door will be a wind of change to blow you into new opportunities. As a courtesy, God is locking people out of your life, people who are like Jonahs. They are deadweight the enemy has placed in your path to make your ship sink.

God is doing this! Your job is to shake the dust from your

feet. As soon as you walk out the door God is closing, your enemies will be locked in your past.

The Bible says, "A wide door for effective work has opened to me, and there are many adversaries" (1 Cor. 16:9, esv). If you believe this word is for you, say, "Yes, Lord," walk out the door, and shake the dust from your feet. Goodness and mercy will follow you all the days of your life. *Selah*!

Today pray…

> *Lord, I pray that in this season You would cause me to be sensitive to doors that You are opening and closing. I call even the closed doors blessings because they are Your way of helping me move forward into new opportunities. I will not be locked in the past, in Jesus's name. Amen.*

_____

_____

_____

_____

_____

_____

_____

_____

_____

_____

DON'T MISS YOUR TIME TO DANCE

To everything there is a season, a time for every purpose under heaven: . . . a time to weep, and a time to laugh; a time to mourn, and a time to dance.

—ECCLESIASTES 3:1, 4

SOMETIMES WE NEED to get with family and friends and just have fun. There is a part of us as humans that needs to be entertained. Don't misunderstand: I don't mix my worship with my entertainment. But I believe God wants us to have enough balance in our lives to have fun. So many believers have frowns on their faces. They walk around with upside-down smiles. This is why so many people do not come to church. They hate dealing with unhappy, miserable church folk.

I believe God has given me grace to endure the storms of being in a frontline warfare ministry through the principle of "keeping it real and having plain, simple fun."

The weapons of your warfare are not carnal. But if you get "too deep," you will never be able to come up for air, and eventually you will become spiritually suffocated. In the natural army soldiers are given breaks during war. It's called R & R, rest and relaxation. They take them out of the war zone and allow them to have fun.

The daughter of one of my best friends from high school got married recently. I have not attended many weddings where I was not the minister officiating the ceremony, and

I had a ball! We all need to have fun sometimes. Jesus performed His first miracle at a wedding.

If you know a minister who is consistently uptight and can't seem to shake it, share this message with him or her. That person may need a break from the war zone. According to Ecclesiastes 3 there is a time to mourn and a time to dance. Don't be so religious that you miss your time to dance. *Selah.*

Today declare...

I will not miss my time to dance!

DO THESE SIGNS FOLLOW YOU?

These signs will accompany those who believe: In My name they will cast out demons; they will speak with new tongues; they will take up serpents; if they drink any deadly thing, it will not hurt them; they will lay hands on the sick, and they will recover."

—MARK 16:17–18

DO YOU BELIEVE the church is walking in the power that God ordained for His body? If you are stuck on this question, look at what God says about it in Ephesians 4:11–12:

> And he gave some, apostles; and some, prophets; and some, evangelists; and some, pastors and teachers; for the *perfecting* of the saints, for the work of the ministry, for the edifying of the body of Christ.
>
> —KJV, EMPHASIS ADDED

In a nutshell God is saying that leaders in the church should be equipping, activating, and imparting what He has put in them to other believers. The Word of the Lord declares that signs should follow believers. Are you a believer? Do these signs follow you?

+ The ministry of casting out devils
+ Speaking in other tongues
+ Walking in the power of God that causes weapons that form against you to never prosper

+ Laying hands on the sick (and seeing them get healed!)

Do you believe that these manifestations are the fruit of being a believer? If not, you should read Mark 16:17–18 again. Many church folk have been less than victorious because they are not walking in the authority of the believer.

Saints, it's time to strap up your boots, take your rightful position in God, and be *all* He has called you to be—victorious!

Today declare . . .

> *I am a believer and others will see the signs. I cast out devils, I speak with other tongues, and I lay hands on the sick and they recover.*

_____

_____

_____

_____

_____

_____

_____

_____

_____

_____

BREAKING BAD HABITS

But this kind does not go out except by prayer and fasting.
—MATTHEW 17:21

～இஇ～

S O MANY PEOPLE are coming to the altar for prayer to break habits. I have found that if you can abstain from, avoid, or fast from a thing for thirty days, you can break the habit. But habits that are not dealt with can create vicious cycles.

The Bible speaks of the prince of the power of the air. He rules over the careless, rebellious, and unbelieving. (See Ephesians 2:2–3.) Every person, place, or thing is connected to a heaven. There are three:

1. First heaven—the sun, moon, and stars, which we can see
2. Second heaven—demonic heavens
3. Third heaven—the throne room of God

The prince of the power of the air abides in the second heaven. In the name of Jesus, I disconnect you right now from any person, place, or thing that is seated in the second heaven. I declare that you are seated in the heaven of heavens with Jesus. Every demonic cycle, habit, or curse is broken off you and the generations of your family.

Sometimes habits break supernaturally through prayer. But more often we have to make changes to break the habit. The worst habit I have ever experienced was an addiction to cigarettes. The power of this habit was that my flesh wanted to smoke, even though I hated the repercussions, which included:

+ Coughing up muck from my lungs
+ Smelling like an ash tray
+ Having my everyday schedule controlled by smoking

There were times when I thought I would kill to get a cigarette, but then I regretted it after I smoked one.

Do you have a person, place, or thing that you cannot shake (and that you know is not good for you)? A word to the wise: not everything that is good *to* you is good *for* you.

Smoking cigarettes was the most difficult thing for me to let go of in my past. It was a demon of death. Every time I smoked a cigarette, it took a day from my life.

I had to take responsibility for my own situation. I had to start somewhere to make a change. So I started by excusing myself from people who indulged in what I was trying to get free from. I could not get free from nicotine with someone blowing smoke in my face every day.

Spiritually speaking, God put a vacuum on the inside of us. I believe that place is empty because we are supposed to fill it with desire and longing for Him. When we allow people, places, or things to fill that space, it is only a matter of time before we self-destruct. Needing anything more than Jesus is not just a bad habit; it is a demonic assignment.

Are you bound by a habit or do you have a secret addiction? Whatever you call it, the answer is simple. Ask Jesus to remove it from your heart and allow Him to come in and fill that empty space.

Today pray...

> *Lord, I ask that You remove from my heart
> anything trying to fill the places that belong to You.
> I commit to fasting and prayer to break the grip of
> these sins off my life. In the name of Jesus, amen.*

_____

_____

_____

_____

_____

_____

_____

_____

_____

_____

_____

_____

_____

_____

SNAKE SEASON

Behold, I give unto you power to tread on serpents
and scorpions, and over all the power of the enemy:
and nothing shall by any means hurt you.

—LUKE 10:19, KJV

I N FLORIDA WHERE I live, spring is snake season. During this time of year I tell my children to always be attentive when they are walking in grassy areas, because when spring arrives, the cold-blooded creatures come out of hibernation.

Just as it is in the natural, so is it in the spirit. Ephesians 5:15 tells us to walk circumspectly, not as fools but as wise, redeeming the time because the days are evil.

It is time for the people of God to watch as well as pray. As I type this, I sense that the "snakes" are coming out of hibernation in the natural and in the spirit. These snakes are those who have hibernated under the warmth of your anointing during the winter and are now suddenly manifesting a different agenda.

These people may have been around you for a while with no apparent problems. But research has proven that some snakes can survive up to two years without a meal.[1] That tells me that a snake can lay low in your life and wait for the opportune moment to bite you. Judas served Jesus for a period of time before his assignment was revealed.

I find it interesting that snakes have no eyelids and never really close their eyes, even when they're sleeping.[2] Be very careful of people who always "see" things on everybody else but have no discernment about their own lives. These are nosy people who get no rest because they are up all night meditating on the calamities of others.

My prayer is that every person in your life with a hidden agenda against you, your children, your job, your business, or your ministry will be exposed and their assignment broken in Jesus's name. Remember, there are two categories of enemies. There are illegitimate enemies the devil sends to trip you up, and there are legitimate enemies that God will allow in your life for a season and a reason. I am addressing the illegitimate enemies.

I bind every trespassing, illegitimate enemy operating in your space in the name of the Lord. I touch and agree with you. In the name of Jesus, we cauterize every two-timing, two-faced, double-tongued, double-minded person in your life.

Know that it is done. God has given us power over the enemy. We need to use it! *Selah*.

Today pray ...

> *Lord, I pray that every person in my life with a hidden agenda against me, my children, my job, my business, and my ministry be exposed and their assignment broken, in Jesus's name. I bind every trespassing, illegitimate enemy operating in my space in the name of the Lord. I cauterize every two-timing, two-faced, double-tongued, double-minded person in my life. In Jesus's name, amen.*

_____

_____

_____

_____

ENEMIES REVEALED

For nothing is secret that will not be revealed, nor anything hidden that will not be known and revealed.

—LUKE 8:17

ONE SUNDAY IN the middle of praise and worship, God dropped the words "seventy-two hours" in my spirit. I told the congregation to speak to every stubborn mountain in their lives, and God would move them in seventy-two hours.

At five o'clock the next morning, my prayer partner and I went into intense intercession. After prayer we both fell into a deep sleep and had similar dreams. I dreamed I was in the Garden of Gethsemane. The setting was 2016, and the people there were tourists. I was hugging a close friend, and we were crying profusely, but our tears were tears of joy.

A man I have known and worked with passed by, looking at us with a smirk on his face. I was surprised because he was supposed to be a friend, so I ran after him to address his attitude toward us. He went to the top of some stairs and stared down at me with the strongest look of hatred I have ever seen. I said to him, "How can you do this when I have helped you?"

Shortly after I woke up from that dream, my prayer partner called to share a dream she had. She dreamed that a huge snake was in her path. No one saw the snake but her. The snake lay in her path as if it could not be seen and tucked its head low. Then small ants came from nowhere and started biting the snake. Because of the sting of the ants, the snake was forced to stand up and be revealed. It was taller than my prayer partner in the dream. As she looked up at the snake, she saw a man on stairs charming the snake. The snake then turned on the charmer and beat him up.

Both dreams were related. Both made reference to revealed enemies (snakes). The man in my dream and the snake in my friend's dream stood on stairs. The stairs represent spiritual wickedness in high places. The small ants biting the huge snake represent "the little foxes spoiling the vine" and "a little leaven leavening the whole lump." Let whoever has ears hear what the Spirit is saying.

The seventy-two hour prophetic word is directly connected to the two dreams. Seventy-two hours is equivalent to three days. On that Sunday I commanded frivolous legal distractions to be moved from my life. Three days later six legal cases were dropped, settled, or resolved in my favor. That happened in one day. Glory to God!

This took place three days after God spoke that word to me. Jesus was raised from the dead in seventy-two hours—and He still has the power to resurrect!

The dreams revealed that to get a breakthrough, enemies/snakes must be exposed and dealt with. I prophesy that just as the snake turned on the charmer, everything used against you will turn on the user and move him or her from your path.

The snakes are coming out of the cracks of your life where they have been hiding during your winter season. Speak to every mountain and command them to be cast into the sea. Snakes don't like sulfur, so I prophesy that "spiritual sulfur" will be released around you and your family to ward off spiritual snakes. God can make everything that was used against you turn around for your good. *Selah.*

Today pray...

> *Lord, I pray that the enemies/snakes in my life will be exposed, dealt with, and removed from my path. I declare that everything used against me will turn around and work for my good. Let spiritual sulfur be released around me and my family to ward off spiritual snakes, in Jesus's name. Amen.*

_____

_____

_____

_____

_____

_____

_____

_____

_____

_____

_____

_____

_____

_____

_____

THE SNAKE IN THE BATHTUB

The thief does not come, except to steal and kill and destroy. I came that they may have life, and that they may have it more abundantly.

—JOHN 10:10

ONE OF THE prophets from my church had a dream not long ago. There was a snake in her bathtub, so she left the bathroom and went into her closet, but there was a bear in the closet. When she left the closet and went into the living room, a lion was there. I do not interpret dreams often, but God quickened my spirit about this one.

The bathtub represents cleansing or deliverance (the church). I have written about the snake season, a time when enemies are exposed for who they are. Many focus on the attacks they receive, when in spiritual reality these attacks are manifestations to expose what has been covertly trying to take them out.

Snakes come into our lives for two reasons:

1. To keep us from getting delivered
2. To take the deliverance we already have

The enemy comes to steal, kill, and destroy. If he can't kill your roots, he will steal your fruit. He does not come to get what you do not have. He wants what you have! He is a thief and a liar. If he is telling you that you will fail, you are on the road to success. It is already yours! The enemy wants to steal your blessing before God reveals it.

The closet represents the things we need to give to God.

The bear is the spirit that keeps these things in the closet. Have you heard of the bear hug? This spirit is like a python that wraps around your chest to squeeze the life out of you.

Jesus came that we might have life (John 10:10). This is where the lion in the living room comes into the picture. Jesus is the lion of the tribe of Judah.

God is in the living room! Church folk fall prey to the most dangerous spiritual traps. They hang out in the "bathtubs" of life and are afraid of the bears in the "closet." We cannot be limited to living in the church building. It can become a stronghold. Bears in the closet bring condemnation and stifle prayer.

The bathtub. The closet. The living room. The church. Our relationship with God. Abundant life! Do not get church mixed up with relationship with God. Whether you are a saint, a "cain't," or an "ain't," God wants you to live the God kind of life—*zóé* (abundant) life! You cannot live "life" in the four walls of the church or in the closet on your face. You live *zóé* life in the living room.

I curse the work of every snake hindering your liberty in Christ, and I bind the power of every bear assigned to squeeze the breath out of your prayer life. Don't be religious because religion denies the power God has already given you. After you've been delivered, live a victorious life in Christ. *Selah.*

Today declare...

> *I curse the work of every snake hindering my liberty in Christ, and I bind the power of every bear assigned to squeeze the breath out of my prayer life, in the name of Jesus. I live a victorious life.*

THE BLESSING IS BIGGER THAN THE GIANTS

The land which we passed through to explore it is a very, very good land. If the LORD delights in us, then He will bring us into this land and give it to us, a land which flows with milk and honey. Only do not rebel against the LORD, nor fear the people of the land because they are bread for us. Their defense is gone from them, and the LORD is with us. Do not fear them

—NUMBERS 14:7–9

YOU MAY HAVE experienced bitterness in years past, but your next season will be sweet. But you can't experience this season of sweetness with stinking thinking.

Get your mind on Jesus! He is the Lord of your breakthrough. Do not cry over the spilled milk of your past. God is taking you into the land of milk and honey. Do not fear the giants that tried to destroy you in the past. The *blessing* is *bigger* than the giants in the land.

Today declare

> *Your blessing is bigger than the giants that tried to take me down in the past. As You bring me into a new season, I will not dwell on past mistakes or past pain. I will look to You.*

_____

_____

_____

_____

_____

_____

_____

_____

_____

_____

_____

_____

_____

_____

_____

_____

_____

_____

_____

_____

_____

_____

_____

_____

_____

_____

BELIEVING FOR A
SEVENFOLD RETURN

But if he be found, he shall restore sevenfold; he
shall give all the substance of his house.

—Proverbs 6:31, kjv

In January 2016 I was unexpectedly invited to speak at a banquet I attended with my twins, who were starting as defensive backs the next day at the Blue-Grey All-American Game for high school athletes. The exclusive, invitation-only game was nationally televised and held in the same stadium where the Jacksonville Jaguars play. NFL veterans were among the coaches, and the top colleges in the country were there scouting out the talent.

I was honored and surprised to be part of the banquet the night before, which NFL coaches and players attended. The banquet put tears in my eyes. Hearing the testimonies of those coaches and players put gas in my spiritual tank and got me fired up.

After that experience God showed me that He was restoring some things the enemy stole from me. It's amazing that once we take our eyes off natural circumstances and situations and recognize who the real thief is, God will make him give back *seven* times what he stole.

I prophecy a *sevenfold* return unto you in Jesus's name! Rest in your restoration. *Selah.*

Today declare...

> *I will rest in my restoration, for God has promised that the thief will restore sevenfold all he has stolen.*

_____

_____

_____

_____

_____

_____

_____

_____

_____

_____

_____

_____

_____

_____

_____

_____

_____

_____

_____

TAKE TIME TO LISTEN

*Therefore, my beloved brothers, let every man be
swift to hear, slow to speak, and slow to anger.*

—JAMES 1:19

I T HAS BEEN eighteen years since I gave birth to my youngest children, and now they are off in college. After much prayer they chose to attend the University of Maryland, where they received full football scholarships. When we were first visiting the school, I set my face to the wall, doing what I call "listening prayer." I didn't want to just take my petitions to God; I needed a word straight from the Lord about my children's future.

Have you ever noticed that the words *listen* and *silent* have the same letters? Sometimes we just need to close our mouths and listen. The blessings of the Lord are running me down and taking me over. I'm not going to let idle words from my mouth shut them down! What about you? Proverbs 17:28 says that even a fool, when he holds his peace, is counted as wise.

In prayer, sometimes we talk so much that we can't hear the voice of God. Let's get before the Lord and hear what He has to say about our situations! Keep a pen and paper handy to write down what He says.

I thank God for a word from the prophet, but there is nothing like a word straight from the heart of God to your spiritual ears. Let whoever has an ear hear what the Spirit is saying to *him*! Take time to listen. *Selah.*

Today declare...

> *Blessings are running me down and taking me over.*
> *I will not let my mouth shut them down. I will be*
> *quick to listen, slow to speak, and slow to anger.*
> *I will take time to listen to what Your Spirit is*
> *saying to me. In Jesus's name, amen.*

_____

_____

_____

_____

_____

_____

_____

_____

_____

_____

_____

_____

_____

_____

_____

THREE LEVELS OF THE WILL OF GOD

I urge you therefore, brothers, by the mercies of God, that you present your bodies as a living sacrifice, holy, and acceptable to God, which is your reasonable service of worship. Do not be conformed to this world, but be transformed by the renewing of your mind, that you may prove what is the good and acceptable and perfect will of God.

—ROMANS 12:1—2

GOD SAYS WE must present our bodies as a living sacrifice, holy and acceptable, which is our reasonable service. And we are not to be conformed to this world but transformed by the renewing of our minds so we will know what the will of God is.

There are three levels of the will of God mentioned in Romans 12:1:

1. Good will (*agathos*), when you're standing by mere faith

2. Acceptable will (*euarestos*), when you have confirmation that you are on the right track

3. Perfect will (*teleios*), when you're smack-dab in the middle of the unquestionable will of God

Desire to be in the *teleios*. Let go of the world and be transformed by the renewing of your mind. Then you will be able to know and walk smack-dab in the undisputable, perfect will of God.

Today pray...

> *God, I accept that there are three levels of Your will for my life. But I desire to be in Your perfect will—the* teleios *of God. Please help me to let go of worldly influences, so that I may be transformed by the renewing of my mind and walk smack-dab in the middle of Your unquestionable will. In Jesus's name, amen.*

_____

_____

_____

_____

_____

_____

_____

_____

_____

_____

_____

_____

_____

A PRAYER FOR THE DREAMERS

The prophet who has a dream, let him tell his dream. And he who has My word, let him speak My word faithfully.

—JEREMIAH 23:28

～❀～

MY SON MICHAEL dreamed that the New York Giants called him to play on the team. He did not play football in college. The same day he had the dream, Tom Coughlin, the head coach of the Giants, called him. He has a Super Bowl ring to prove it.

Five years ago I had a dream that I was to become an elected official. Within three months I received almost 93,000 votes and won the seat I was running for. Today I'm still dreaming! God is doing great things for those who trust Him. Remember, without vision (or a dream) people perish! *Selah.*

Today pray…

> *Father, I thank You for sweet sleep, divine rest, and a Holy Ghost download during my sleep life. Give me direction, correction, warning, comfort, and protection. Minister healing and deliverance to my soul, spirit, and body. May my visions, dreams, thoughts, daydreams, and images be fruitful and blessed when I tap into the dream realm. Delete every file or program of distraction from my soul. Clear my spirit of any blockages to a wholesome dream life. I commit to think on things that are true, honest, just, pure, lovely, of good report,*

and full of virtue and praise. Anoint me between sleeping and waking up. Download Your will to me as I rest. Amen.

_____

_____

_____

_____

_____

_____

_____

_____

_____

_____

_____

_____

_____

_____

_____

_____

_____

_____

THE THOUSANDFOLD BLESSING

*For I, the LORD your God, am a jealous God, visiting the
iniquity of the fathers on the children to the third and fourth
generation of them who hate Me, and showing lovingkindness to
thousands of them who love Me and keep My commandments.*

—EXODUS 20:5–6

GENERATIONAL BLESSINGS ARE greater than generational
curses! Exodus 20:5 tells us that family curses go
back three or four generations. But keep reading. Exodus
20:6 declares that the blessings *go forward* for a thousand
generations. My family has been through a lot. But Jesus!

No matter how many attacks you get in life, confess that
your seed is *blessed*! I release the favor of God over your seed.
Don't look back. Move forward. Pray this confession out
loud, and share it with friends who need to be encouraged
concerning their children.

Today pray…

> *Father, in the name of Jesus, I renounce every
> bloodline curse. I press forward and receive the
> thousandfold blessing over my generation and the
> generations of my family that follow. My children
> will not experience the attacks of my past. My
> seed is contagiously blessed. Lord, I believe You
> are opening doors that no man can deny. My sons
> and daughters will walk through these doors, and
> wherever the soles of their feet shall touch, they*

will prosper because the land will yield unlimited increase to them. Favor is divinely deposited to my bloodline! My family is moving forward in God. Amen.

COMBATING THE SPIRIT OF FEAR

For God has not given us the spirit of fear, but of power, and love, and self-control.

—2 TIMOTHY 1:7

I HAVE RECEIVED MANY prayer requests over the past few days. I have read every one of them, and in 95 percent of the cases, fear was listed as the giant keeping the person from reaching his or her promised land.

If you need to overcome fear in your life, declare these confessions as often as you need to. And read Psalm 91 to remind yourself of the confidence you can have in God.

Today declare...

> I abide in God's secret place, where my mind is fixed and void of doublemindedness.
>
> I confidently trust in and lean on God.
>
> I am delivered from every trap of the enemy. I'm under the covering of my Father.
>
> I do not fear night terrors or attacks by day that send evil plots or the slanderous arrows of the wicked.
>
> I renounce pestilence that stalks in darkness or sudden-death noonday surprises.

A thousand may fall to one side and ten thousand to the other, but no harm will come nigh me.

No plague or calamity shall come close to where I live.

The Lord has loosed angels to accompany, defend, and preserve me and my household.

I renounce the spirit of bondage that ignites fear. If God is for me, who can be against me?

I will not be afraid, ashamed, alarmed, humiliated, disgraced, frightened, or terrorized.

Roots of rejection, rebellion, jealousy, loneliness, and insecurity have no place in my heart.

I will never fear man. The fear of God is my portion. Amen.

RELEASING THE
SPIRIT OF VALOR

*Be strong and of good courage. Do not tremble or be dismayed,
for the LORD your God is with you wherever you go.*

—JOSHUA 1:9

GOD HAS NOT given you a spirit of fear. You and your seed shall inherit the promise! God will not take you into the promised land and leave your children in the wilderness. Move forward! The spirit of valor is coming upon you. In the midst of your greatest attack, you will have sweet sleep and divine rest. *Selah.*

Today declare...

> *A spirit of valor is coming upon me in the name of Jesus. No demon in hell will stop me or my children from inheriting the promise. Even when under attack, I will have sweet sleep and divine rest. In Jesus's name, amen.*

_____

_____

_____

_____

_____

_____

_____

_____

_____

_____

_____

_____

_____

_____

_____

_____

_____

_____

_____

_____

_____

_____

_____

GOD WILL SET YOU UP FOR GOOD

We know that all things work together for good to those who love God, to those who are called according to His purpose.
—ROMANS 8:28

WE HAVE TO shift with what God is doing. While in prayer recently, I saw these words: "I'm not pressed. It's a setup!" Even when the devil attempts to set you up for evil, God will set you up for good. All things work together for the good of those who love God and are called according to His purpose. Stay focused on His promises. Don't let anything distract you. God is working things out for your good.

Today declare...

God is setting me up for good!

_____

_____

_____

_____

_____

_____

_____

_____

_____

_____

_____

_____

_____

_____

_____

_____

_____

_____

_____

_____

_____

_____

_____

_____

_____

_____

_____

_____

_____

_____

_____

PERSECUTION IS A PATH TO PROMOTION

*When a man's ways please the LORD, He makes
even his enemies to be at peace with him.*

—PROVERBS 16:7

❧

THERE ARE THREE categories of haters—the naysayer, the gainsayer, and the soothsayer. All of them are rooted and grounded in speaking negative words.

The naysayer has the "spirit of no" in his or her mouth and continually seeds it into your life to keep you in the prison of what you can "never" do.

The gainsayer denies truth with the ulterior motive of tearing you down. This spirit gets pleasure out of lying and has no intention or desire to receive or know truth. It actually gains from others' pain.

The soothsayer is one who speaks through the demonic power of a third eye and knowingly releases words that do not originate from God.

Many are the afflictions of the righteous but God delivers us from them all (Ps. 34:19). The Egyptians afflicted the children of Israel with strong yokes of bondage. They held them down. But the more the Israelites were held down, the more they prospered. This is a sign that God is with a person. They may wobble and get knocked down, but they never stay down!

The way to promotion is persecution. Stop crying about

your challenges. God is up to something bigger than your enemies are.

Your haters will help catapult you into your destiny. Once you are released to your next level of promotion, even your enemies will say, "Only God!"

Stay in the right spirit. When your ways please God, even your enemies will be at peace with you. After all, who wants to continually exert energy holding someone down who always gets up again?

Today declare…

> *I may get knocked down, but I will not stay down. God is with me. My promotion comes through persecution.*

_____

_____

_____

_____

_____

_____

_____

_____

_____

_____

_____

CONFESS THE WORD OVER YOUR SEED

I have been young, and now am old; yet I have not seen the righteous forsaken, nor their offspring begging bread.

—PSALM 37:25

OUR CHILDREN ARE hungry for God! Feed them the Word.

I have seen God work so many miracles for my children that I want to encourage you to stand in faith for God to bless your seed. Isaiah 49:23 declares that those who wait on the Lord will not be ashamed (damned or cursed). God will complete the work He has begun in your children. No weapons formed against you shall prosper.

I have been young and now I'm getting older, and I have never seen the righteous forsaken nor their seed begging bread. As often as you feel led, make this confession over your seed and trust God to bring them into their place of destiny.

Today stand in faith for your children...

> *I repent of the things of the past and present that have opened "doors of trouble" for my children [name each child].*
>
> *I plead the blood over the navel(s) of my child(ren) where life first flowed. The work that God has begun He will finish!*

Every destiny devourer is overthrown. The power of peer pressure and ungodly association is broken from my seed. Negative declarations over my children are erased. I speak sweet sleep over them when they sleep at night. The spirit of the world is bound, and the discernment of my children is not dark. My children shall rise up, demand room to live, and call me blessed. Blessings, abundance, and favor will be their portion forever. My children are healthy, wealthy, and wise. They shall possess the gates of their enemies. This is the heritage of my seed for a thousand generations. In Jesus's name, amen.

_____

_____

_____

_____

_____

_____

_____

_____

_____

_____

_____

_____

STAND IN THE GAP FOR
THE NEXT GENERATION

*I sought for a man among them who would build up the hedge and
stand in the gap before Me for the land so that I would not destroy it.*

—EZEKIEL 22:30

T HE POWER OF posterity (what we leave for the next
generation) is more precious than prosperity (what we
can accumulate while we are living). *Selah.* Pause and think
on that.

We need to stand in the gap for the next generation. At
the end of April, I called on intercessors to touch and agree
for young people who were:

+ Being promoted to the next grade
+ Graduating from one level of education to the next
  (such as from elementary school to middle school)
+ Graduating from high school
+ Graduating from college
+ Entering into or graduating from a higher level of
  education (such as law school or medical school)

We need to pray for young people moving forward in
their education because even though education is power,
an educated mind void of the mind of Christ is dangerous.
Here is a prayer I speak over my children. Declare it over the

young people in your life. And as you do, know that I am standing in agreement with you.

Today pray for the next generation...

> *Father God, in the name of Jesus, I stand in agreement with Apostle Daniels. I plead the blood of Jesus over the generation You are raising up today. Protect them from the traps that are laid before them. Provide for them physically, spiritually, financially, mentally, and emotionally. I declare that their countenances will be brilliant and shine for Your glory. Let uncommon favor be their portion and every place the soles of their feet touch be subdued. May they go forth and be educated and anointed to possess the land. Amen.*

_____

_____

_____

_____

_____

_____

_____

_____

_____

_____

NEW REALMS

But we all, seeing the glory of the Lord with unveiled faces, as in a mirror, are being transformed into the same image from glory to glory by the Spirit of the Lord.

—2 CORINTHIANS 3:18

I HEAR THE LORD saying, "New realms." Many people are striving for their next level, but God wants to take them into a new realm in the spirit.

The thief on the cross did not go to his next level. Based on where he was, his next level was hell. But then he met Jesus and stepped into another realm. Titus 3:5 says we are not saved by works but by God's mercy.

Believers must understand the difference between "levels" and "realms." A level is what you ascend to in an elevator; you can go from one floor to another. There are a limited number of floors, or levels, in a building that the elevator can reach. However, there is not a limit on the number of spiritual realms.

There is a saying that "there is a devil on every level." This is true, but a devil cannot affect you when God takes you into a new realm. Stop struggling with enemies from level to level and break out into a new realm. Levels take you up. A new realm breaks you out!

There were times in the Bible when people tried to lay hands on Jesus and He was just not there anymore. (See John 8:59.) *Glory!* I prophesy that you are "not there anymore"! Wherever you were when your enemies tried to touch you, the situation has rolled off you like water off a duck's back. Why? Because you are not in the place they thought you were!

Receive this word, forgive your transgressors, and be delivered into your next realm. *Selah.*

Today declare...

> *I am not just going to another level; I am going to a whole new realm. I am breaking out!*

_____

_____

_____

_____

_____

_____

_____

_____

_____

_____

_____

_____

_____

_____

THE KING OF PRIDE

Humble yourselves under the mighty hand of
God, that He may exalt you in due time.

—1 PETER 5:6

THERE IS A strongman that rules over personal lives, families, businesses, churches, and the government. This spirit is mentioned in Job 41. It operates behind the scenes, shutting down businesses, destroying relationships, and splitting churches every day. The name of this spirit is Leviathan, and he is the king of pride.

The definition of pride is to have a high opinion of one's own dignity, importance, merit, or superiority. It is good to be proud of accomplishments, but we must beware of thinking more of ourselves than we ought to (Rom 12:3).

The power of pride is that it operates covertly in the lives of good, innocent people. As for me, I renounce pride. I refuse to allow it to hinder my blessings. James 4:6 says that "God resists the proud but gives grace to the humble." Humility is the key to real power. When we humble ourselves under the mighty hand of God, He exalts us in due season.

It is time for promotion. Renounce pride!

Today pray…

> Lord, I renounce pride and humble myself under
> Your mighty hand. I refuse to allow pride to hinder
> my blessings and promotion, in the name of Jesus.

*I look forward to the promotion that comes from
You. Amen.*

STEWARD "SHIP" IS THE VESSEL OF TRUE PROSPERITY

From the days of your fathers you have gone away from My ordinances and have not kept them. Return to Me, and I will return to you, says the LORD of Hosts.

—MALACHI 3:7

No MATTER HOW much you have coming in, the locust, palmer worm, and canker worm are waiting to devour what you have. Don't be a steward whose pocket has holes in it. When you don't bring the Lord His portion, you will find that you "have sown much, and harvested little. You eat, but you do not have enough; you drink, but you are not filled with drink; you clothe yourselves, but no one is warm" (Hag. 1:6).

Don't forget the house of the Lord. God wants to bless you going out and coming in. He rebukes the devourer for those who don't rob Him. There really is a Grinch, but he is called the devourer. He creeps into our houses over commercial holidays to eat up our increase.

Let those who have an ear hear what the Spirit is saying. *Selah.*

Today declare...

> *I am blessed going out and coming in. The devourer has been rebuked.*

FAST-FORWARD

Believe in the LORD your God, so shall ye be established;
believe his prophets, so shall ye prosper.

—2 CHRONICLES 20:20, KJV

T HE BIBLE DECLARES that if we believe in God, we will be established, but if we believe the prophet, we will prosper (be pushed forward). I believe there are some people who will be "fast-forwarded"! This means that some who have been held back will now be supernaturally pushed forward at a Holy Ghost rate of speed. Those who are fast-forwarded will have a testimony about which people will say, "Look at where they are now in comparison to where they used to be!"

Exhortation and confirmation are key in walking out prophetic words that have been spoken over our lives. People need to be exhorted because everyday challenges in life can easily tire us out. We need confirmations because things are established out of the mouths of two or three witnesses. When words of confirmation and exhortation enter the hearts of God's people, revival fire will surely be sparked. This fire will spark like the wick at the end of a stick of dynamite, releasing *dunamis* power and deliverance!

Today declare…

> *I have been fast-forwarded. Because I believe in*
> *God and trust His prophets, I will succeed. I will*
> *be pushed forward into the greater things of God.*

LORD, OPEN OUR EYES

And he said, "Do not be afraid, for there are more with us than with them." Then Elisha prayed, "LORD, open his eyes and let him see."

—2 KINGS 6:16–17

GOD TOLD ABRAHAM that his seed would be as numerous as the stars in the sky, as far as he could see (Gen. 15:5). When Elisha's servant was afraid of the enemies rising up against them, the prophet prayed, "Lord, open his eyes so that he can see that there is more working for us behind the scenes than against us." What we see is temporal. What we cannot see is eternal. We must open our eyes to the things that are eternal.

The first step to opening our eyes is separating ourselves from people who are not who they say they are. They bring too much warfare. You can't bind the devil while you're hanging out with him. Once you get rid of him, you will see more clearly.

Today pray…

> *Lord, open my spiritual eyes to see what You see. Show me Your hand working behind the scenes so that I can see and believe that there are more for me than against me. Thank You that Your promises for me extend far beyond what my eyes can see. Amen.*

A PRAYER FOR YOUR CHILDREN

And the LORD said unto Moses, Write this for a memorial in a book, and rehearse it in the ears of Joshua: for I will utterly put out the remembrance of Amalek from under heaven.

—EXODUS 17:14, KJV

THE AMALEKITES WERE considered eternal enemies of God and His people. They made war with the Israelites for generations, often attacking them for no reason at all. When the Israelites were coming out of Egypt, exhausted and weary, the Amalekites attacked the stragglers at the rear, many of whom were women and children (Deut. 25:17–18). Then in 1 Samuel 30 the Bible says they burned Ziklag (David's camp) and took the women and the children captive.

God told Moses to rehearse victory over Amalek in the ears of Joshua (we do this through the Word of God) because He would wipe out the remembrance of this enemy. God was true to His Word, and the people of Amalek no longer exist. But the spirit of Amalek is still alive, and it is assigned against our children.

Modern-day Amalekites include:

+ Sexual perversion
+ Sexually transmitted diseases (STDs)
+ Teenage pregnancy
+ Misdemeanor or felony criminal activity
+ Mental attacks and disorders

+ Illiteracy/dropping out of school
+ Antichrist leadership in the school system
+ Antichrist governmental legislation
+ Demonic political indoctrination
+ Child molestation/sexual predators
+ Kidnapping and murder
+ Peer pressure
+ Drug addiction
+ Racism
+ Poverty
+ Child abuse
+ Suicide and depression
+ Insecurity
+ Bullying
+ Hopelessness
+ Gang-related activity
+ Human trafficking
+ Unemployment
+ Failure
+ Socially or politically incited demonic terrorism on school campuses

(If you think of some Amalekites assigned against children that are not listed, add them to your prayer list.)

To resist these demonic attacks against the next generation, "bind" the assignments of Amalek and "loose" these godly manifestations over your seed and any other young people in your life.

Today pray for the next generation...

> Father God, in the name of Jesus, I touch and agree with Apostle Daniels that the following manifestations will be my children's portion. My children will be:
>
> Prayerful, having hearts sensitive to constant contact with God (1 Thess. 5:17)
>
> Faithful, having hearts filled with love and faith that will work for them and bless others (Prov. 3:3)
>
> Grateful, having hearts filled with gratitude and thanksgiving (Eph. 5:20)
>
> Self-disciplined, having lives that are disciplined and prudent (Prov. 1:3)
>
> Passionate for God, having hearts that hunger for God's purpose and presence in their lives (Ps. 63:8)
>
> Willing and diligent workers, having minds that value hard work and understand its benefits (Col. 3:23)
>
> Hopeful, having hearts that hope in God for all things (Rom. 5:5)
>
> Responsible, having hearts and minds to carry the load of life and be faithful to their portion (Gal. 6:5)
>
> Humble, having spirits void of ungodly pride and jealousy but that promote humility in success (Titus 3:2)
>
> Joyful, having souls that experience joy that can be given only by the Holy Spirit (1 Thess. 1:6)
>
> Peaceful, having minds that rest despite the mental warfare released by the world (Rom. 14:19)

Courageous, having courageous character and mind-sets that fear God and not man (Deut. 31:6)

Respectful, having personalities that give and receive respect (1 Pet. 2:17)

Pure, having pure hearts before God and manifesting this trait when making decisions (Ps. 51:10)

Honest, having integrity and honesty that release virtue and protection (Ps. 25:21)

Loving, having hearts filled with love that permeates their souls by God's Spirit (Eph. 5:2)

Saved, with their heads covered with the helmet of salvation to release eternal peace (2 Tim. 2:10)

_____

_____

_____

_____

_____

_____

_____

_____

_____

_____

BIND THE SPIRIT OF THE HEADHUNTERS

*The LORD will cause your enemies who rise up against
you to be defeated before you; they will come out against
you one way and flee before you seven ways.*

—DEUTERONOMY 28:7

ONE MORNING I heard the Lord say, "Bind the spirit of the headhunters." God was talking not about professionals who help people find jobs but about spiritual darkness assigned to cut off the head.

Spiritual headhunters go after the heads of families, the heads of churches, and even the heads of nations. But as the mother of three sons, I believe there's a particular assignment against the male seed, especially young black men. You need only to look at the news to know how vicious the enemy's attacks against young black men are. The enemy wants to destroy their purpose, but the devil is a liar. Let the mighty men of valor rise up!

As people of God, we are called to be the head and not the tail, and headhunters want to cut off our authority, our faith, and who God has called us to be. Fight back in prayer.

Today pronounce double grace on the male seed. And refuse to let the headhunters cut off your portion. *Selah.*

Today declare...

> *The enemy will not be able to cut off my faith, my authority, or my calling. I am above and not beneath, the head and not the tail. Everything I put my hands to do will prosper. I pronounce double grace on the male seed, and decree and declare that the mighty men of valor will arise. Anoint their heads with oil, let their cup overflow, and let goodness and mercy follow them all the days of their lives. In Jesus's name, amen.*

IT'S TIME FOR A NEW
LEVEL OF WARFARE

*For the weapons of our warfare are not carnal, but mighty
through God to the pulling down of strongholds.*

—2 CORINTHIANS 10:4

I FEEL LED TO share more about demonic headhunters.
Tribes of headhunters existed until the early 1960s
when they were evangelized by American missionaries.
Head-hunting tribal warriors were cannibalistic blood-
drinkers and flesh-eaters who wore the heads of their victims
around their necks. The highest honor of a young warrior
was to wear the head of a king around his neck. They put tat-
toos on their faces to show how many kings they had killed.
They also pierced their ears with animal horns to denote the
blood sacrifices.[1]

The devil is killing kings every day. Believers are children of
the King, heirs of God and joint heirs with Christ. Darkness
is targeting godly families, ministries, and community
leadership.

Today young gang members tattoo their faces with
tears to record the lives they have taken in their initiation
process. Young people pierce their ears with huge hornlike
paraphernalia to follow a fad. It is amazing to me how
demonic traditions travel through time and become fads.
These fetishes (demonic observances) will operate behind the
scenes until our young people are evangelized. Missionaries

evangelized the Konyak people (who were headhunters) before the sixties. Who will evangelize our young people in America today?

The young people are not the headhunters, but those spirits are operating behind the scenes. The weapons of our warfare *are not carnal!* It is time to go to another level of warfare. It is time for the saints to be perfected for the work of the ministry. *Selah.*

Today declare...

> *The weapons of my warfare are not carnal but are mighty through God to pull down strongholds. I choose to be perfected for the work of the ministry. I choose to stand in the gap and intercede for the next generation.*

GET IN THE GAME

*Therefore submit yourselves to God. Resist
the devil, and he will flee from you.*

—JAMES 4:7

I WAS IN SCOTTSDALE, Arizona, when Muhammad Ali, the greatest boxing champion of all time, died. As great a boxer as Muhammad Ali was, even he lost some fights. But there is no shame in losing because it means you're in the game.

As Christians, we win in the end. But there will be battles along the way. We can't sit them out for fear we'll lose. Resist the enemy, and he *will* flee. Don't give room (access or an entry point) to your enemies. Hide yourself in God. *Selah.*

Today pray…

> *Lord, I hide myself in You. I will not fear the adversary, for greater is He who is in me than he who is in the world. You have given me power to tread on serpents and scorpions and over all the power of the enemy, and nothing shall by any means harm me. I am Your servant. I choose to get in the game because I know that when I resist the devil, he will flee. Thank You for the victory! In Jesus's name, amen.*

_____

_____

_____

_____

_____

_____

_____

_____

_____

_____

_____

_____

_____

_____

_____

_____

_____

_____

_____

_____

_____

_____

KEEP YOUR FOCUS

*Let us look to Jesus, the author and finisher of our faith, who for
the joy that was set before Him endured the cross, despising the
shame, and is seated at the right hand of the throne of God.*

—HEBREWS 12:2

BE FREE FROM distractions. Distractions can be subliminal, peripheral, from yesterday, or about tomorrow. The opposite of distraction is focus. Be focused on the destiny God has for you. Rest in Him. *Selah.*

Today declare…

> *I will keep my eyes on Jesus. I will stay focused on the destiny God has for me and rest in Him as He accomplishes His purpose in my life.*

_____

_____

_____

_____

_____

_____

_____

_____

_____

_____

_____

_____

_____

_____

_____

_____

_____

_____

_____

_____

_____

_____

_____

_____

_____

_____

_____

_____

_____

_____

TELL GOD YES

For many are called, but few are chosen.
—MATTHEW 22:14

ﻬ

MANY ARE CALLED but few are chosen. Answering the call qualifies you to be chosen. It is a terrible thing to die never fulfilling what you were born to do. Tell God yes to His will and accept your calling. Then step into the land of the chosen.

Be a blessing. Preach! Teach! Prophesy! Deliver! Win souls! *Selah.*

Today declare...

> *I say yes to You and choose to walk in the fullness of Your calling on my life. I will not die never having fulfilled the thing You created me to do. I choose to be a blessing and win souls for Your glory. Amen.*

_____

_____

_____

_____

_____

_____

_____

YOU ARE NOT ALONE

*Still, I have preserved seven thousand men in Israel
for Myself, all of whose knees have not bowed to
Baal and whose mouths have not kissed him.*

—1 KINGS 19:18

YOU ARE NOT the only one serving God. The enemy wants
to make you think you're all alone, but there are more
for you than there can ever be against you. It may seem as
if everyone around you has forsaken God, but God has a
remnant. God has preserved seven thousand in Israel who
have not bowed their knee to Baal.

You are not the only one. But remember, one can put a
thousand to flight, and two can put ten thousand to flight.
That means even if it were just you and me, we could still put
ten thousand to flight. *Selah.*

Today declare…

> *The devil is a liar. I am not the only one out here
> serving God. I am not alone in warfare. There
> are more with me than there are against me. I am
> victorious in Jesus's name, amen.*

_____

_____

_____

_____

_____

_____

_____

_____

_____

_____

_____

_____

_____

_____

_____

_____

_____

_____

_____

_____

_____

_____

_____

_____

_____

_____

_____

WHOM ARE YOU LISTENING TO?

Then Jezebel sent a messenger to Elijah, saying, "So let the gods do to me and more also, if I do not make your life as the life of one of them by tomorrow about this time." When he saw that she was serious, he arose and ran for his life to Beersheba.

—1 KINGS 19:2–3

ELIJAH SLEW FOUR hundred fifty prophets of Baal. He stood on Mount Carmel in the fullness of the power of God, but then after this victory, one witch named Jezebel sent a word that made him run for his life. One word struck fear in his heart after all God had done.

The enemy will use anything to keep you from the call of God. He will use naysayers, soothsayers, and gainsayers to tell you that you can't be what God called you to be. Don't listen to them! Rebuke them in the name of Jesus.

You cannot allow anyone to deter you from doing what God told you to do. A lot of people wondered why I chose to run for political office. It's because I heard the call of God. God is sending out a clarion call to His people. You may be called to have a dental practice or a law firm. You may be called to serve God as a pastor, politician, or athlete. In whatever capacity God calls you to, serve. Don't let that Jezebel spirit stop you. *Selah.*

Today pray…

Lord, let my confidence always be in You. I bind every naysayer, gainsayer, and soothsayer, the threefold cord that would say I can't be what You called me to be or do what You called me to do. I break every negative word spoken over my life. I say yes to Your calling. I choose to follow You, in Jesus's name, amen.

_____

_____

_____

_____

_____

_____

_____

_____

_____

_____

_____

_____

_____

_____

SHUT YOUR EARS TO
DREAM KILLERS

*And you shall anoint Jehu, the son of Nimshi, to be king
over Israel, and you shall anoint Elisha, the son of Shaphat
of Abel Meholah, to be prophet in your place.*

—1 KINGS 19:16

EVERY TIME THE people of God cried out to Him, God raised up a deliverer. You may be one of those deliverers, but if you don't shut your eyes and ears to dream killers, you won't accomplish your purpose.

Elijah had defeated four hundred fifty prophets of Baal, but as soon as Jezebel threatened to kill him, the prophet ran for the hills. Then watch what happened. After Elijah fled for his life, God met Elijah in a cave and gave him instructions to go to the Wilderness of Damascus and anoint Elijah to be prophet *in his place.* If you don't do whatever God is calling you to do, He will anoint someone to take your place. Whatever the call is, you have to answer it. *Selah.*

Today pray...

> *Lord, help me to shut my eyes and ears to dream killers. I want to do all You've called me to do and be all You've called me to be. I say yes. I hold nothing back from You. I want to do Your will. In Jesus's name, amen.*

_____

_____

_____

_____

_____

_____

_____

_____

_____

_____

_____

_____

_____

_____

_____

_____

_____

_____

_____

_____

_____

_____

_____

_____

_____

_____

THROW YOUR HANDS
UP IN PRAISE!

Out of the mouth of babes and nursing infants You have ordained strength because of Your enemies, to silence the enemy and the avenger.

—PSALM 8:2

SOMEONE HAD A dream about me. The person said in the dream I was walking in confidence, and then all of a sudden a big black bird swooped down and I threw my hands up in the air. The person thought I was giving up, but she didn't know that I have a tendency to throw my hands up when I praise God. When trouble comes, I praise the Lord.

When the enemy sends trouble your way, throw your hands up in praise. Many are the afflictions of the righteous, but God delivers us from them all. Whatever you're going through right now, it cannot stifle, it cannot stop, it cannot shut down the call of God on your life. Answer trouble with praise.

Today pray…

> Lord, let Your praise be ever on my lips. When trouble comes, I choose to respond with praise because praise silences the enemy. Thank You, Lord! You are worthy to be praised! Amen.

_____

_____

_____

_____

_____

_____

_____

_____

_____

_____

_____

_____

_____

_____

_____

_____

_____

_____

_____

_____

_____

_____

_____

_____

_____

_____

_____

THE GATES OF HELL WILL NOT PREVAIL

*And I tell you that you are Peter, and on this rock I will build
My church, and the gates of Hades shall not prevail against
it. I will give you the keys of the kingdom of heaven, and
whatever you bind on earth shall be bound in heaven, and
whatever you loose on earth shall be loosed in heaven.*

—MATTHEW 16:18–19

AFTER YOU DO something good in God, all of hell is
going to come and try to stop you from doing what God
is calling you to do. But the gates of hell shall not prevail
against you if you are part of the body of Christ.

The Bible says to present your body a living sacrifice, holy
and acceptable, which is your reasonable service (Rom. 12:1).
It's the least you can do. Don't be conformed. Don't be like
anybody else. You need to be who God called you to be.
Let God change you by the renewing of your mind. Then
do what God has called you to do. When you walk in your
purpose, the enemy may come in like a flood against you, but
the Lord will raise up a standard against him. *Selah.*

Today declare…

> *I will not be intimidated by the enemy. I will
> pursue the calling on my life because I know that
> greater is He who is in me than he who is in the*

world. I refuse to be discouraged, but I will rejoice in the Lord, for He is my strength. Amen.

_____

_____

_____

_____

_____

_____

_____

_____

_____

_____

_____

_____

_____

_____

_____

_____

_____

_____

_____

_____

JOIN FORCES

And if someone might overpower another by himself, two together can withstand him. A threefold cord is not quickly broken.

—ECCLESIASTES 4:12

THERE IS A demonic threefold cord of me, myself, and I. Remember, God has more resources than you do. He has more servants than Kimberly Daniels or T. D. Jakes or Joyce Meyer. He has more servants than the pastor and elders in your church or even in your city.

We spend too much time separated in our little cubicles. God wants us to join forces. He wants us to link up and unite. If one can put a thousand to flight, two can put ten thousand to flight. *Selah.*

Today pray...

> *Lord, let me not think more highly of myself than I ought. Let me not think I have no one to lean on in prayer, in ministry, or in warfare. I choose to link up with others because if one can put a thousand to flight, two can put ten thousand to flight. I choose to walk in unity with others in Your body. In Jesus's name, amen.*

_____

_____

_____

ARISE AND EAT

The angel of the LORD came again a second time and touched him and said, "Arise and eat, because the journey is too great for you." He arose and ate and drank and went in the strength of that food forty days and forty nights to Horeb, the mountain of God.

—1 Kings 19:7–8

God came to Elijah while he was under the juniper tree and brought him water and food. Elijah ate and drank, and then he lay down and fell asleep. The Lord woke him up and told him to eat again "because the journey is too great for you." The Bible says that food kept Elijah for forty days and forty nights until he reached Horeb, the mountain of God.

Let whoever has ears hear what the Spirit is saying. God has brought you supernatural provision, and He wants you to arise and "eat" the Word of God because you can't handle the things ahead of you without Him. There are some things coming to America, there are some things coming to your church, and there are some things coming into your life that you won't be able to handle if you don't eat.

If you don't have the Word inside of you, when life squeezes you, you won't have anything to give back. But if you're filled with the Word, when life squeezes you, the Word is going to come out, and it's going to make a difference in someone's life. Eat the Word. *Selah.*

Today pray...

> *Lord, I thank You for Your Word. I choose to eat of it and be filled. I thank You for Your supernatural provision to prepare me for what is ahead. In Jesus's name, amen.*

_____

_____

_____

_____

_____

_____

_____

_____

_____

_____

_____

_____

_____

_____

_____

_____

_____

THE ANOINTING
BELONGS TO GOD

You did not choose Me, but I chose you, and appointed you, that you
should go and bear fruit, and that your fruit should remain, that
the Father may give you whatever you ask Him in My name.

—JOHN 15:16

IN 2 KINGS 2, when Elijah was about to be caught up, he asked Elisha what he wanted, and he said, "I want a double portion of the anointing on your life." Elisha had seen Elijah raise the dead. He had seen him walk on water. And he wanted a double portion of the anointing that rested on his life.

Elijah promised Elisha that he would receive a double portion of his anointing if Elisha saw him when he was taken up to heaven. But on the day he was to be taken up, Elijah kept telling Elisha that he didn't have to follow him. Elisha said, "The devil is a liar!" He knew what God said he was supposed to have. It didn't matter what Elijah said or did; Elisha wasn't going to miss his mantle. Elisha knew the anointing didn't belong to Elijah; it belonged to God, and Elijah just walked in it. So Elisha was there when Elijah was caught up. And he picked up the prophet's mantle after he was gone and received a double portion of the anointing on Elijah's life.

Don't let anyone keep you from what God has for you— not the apostle, the prophet, the pastor, the evangelist, or the teacher. People don't call you; God does. He may have you follow someone for a season to receive an impartation, but that person isn't the one responsible for the anointing on your life; God is. *Selah.*

Today declare…

> *I will not live my life trying to be approved of or accepted by people. You are the one who called me, and I will follow You as I pursue the call on my life. I will not let people cause me to miss my mantle. I will fulfill my destiny in You.*

_____

_____

_____

_____

_____

_____

_____

_____

_____

_____

_____

_____

_____

_____

DON'T TAKE YOUR ANOINTING TO THE GRAVE

So Elisha died, and they buried him. Now Moabite raiders would enter the land in the spring. As they were burying a man, they saw raiders. So they threw the man into the tomb of Elisha. When the man touched the bones of Elisha, he came to life and stood on his feet.

—2 KINGS 13:20–21

A YEAR AFTER HE had died, Elisha's bones still had resurrection power in them. That's how powerful the anointing was on Elisha's life. But let me ask you something: Why did Elisha take the anointing on his life to his grave? Why did someone have to throw a dead man into a grave in order for him to be raised to life? The anointing on his life should have been operating in somebody.

I ran for political office because I didn't want to take the anointing to my grave. I believe in being a shaker and a mover in whatever God has called me to do. Like the apostle Paul, I want to be able to say, "I have fought a good fight, I have finished my course, I have kept the faith" (2 Tim. 4:7, KJV). Come out of limbo and be all that God called you to be. Don't take your anointing to the grave.

Today declare…

> I will not take the anointing on my life to the grave.
> I will do all You put in my heart and mind to do. I
> will follow You where You lead and become a mover

and a shaker in the realm to which You assign me. Thank You for Your plans for me. I know they are good plans, to prosper me and not to harm me, to bring me to an expected end. In Jesus's name, amen.

STAY IN THE SPIRIT

*For the weapons of our warfare are not carnal, but mighty
through God to the pulling down of strongholds.*
—2 CORINTHIANS 10:4

WHEN YOU ARE standing with enemies who are spiritually ignorant, stay in the Spirit because you'll lose them there. Carnally minded people will want to take you into their intellectual realm or into the realms where they think they can overshadow you or override you. But stay in the Spirit.

Yes, you have to be professional. Yes, you have to operate in the natural aspect of what you're called to do. But stay in the spirit realm, and you will lose your enemies because the carnal mind cannot understand and discern the things of the Spirit. You can take the lawyer of lawyers into the spirit realm, and if he is carnally minded, he will be lost because he does not understand the things of the Spirit.

Don't fight flesh with flesh. The weapons of your warfare are not carnal. They are mighty through God to the pulling down of strongholds. That's the secret to success when you're dealing with the world. Stay in the Spirit. Maintain your position. Stand in the realm God has called you to stand in. *Selah.*

Today declare…

> *The weapons of my warfare are not carnal but
> mighty through God. I will not fight flesh with flesh.*

I will stay in the spirit and allow You to fight my battles. In Jesus's name, amen.

_____

_____

_____

_____

_____

_____

_____

_____

_____

_____

_____

_____

_____

_____

_____

_____

_____

GOD IS GIVING YOU
HELP ON THE WAY

*Beloved, I wish above all things that thou mayest prosper
and be in health, even as thy soul prospereth.*

—3 JOHN 2, KJV

THE WORD TRANSLATED "prosper" in 3 John 2 is *euodoó*
in the Greek. It means to be on the road to the promise
or having help on the way. That means you may not be where
you need to be. You may not have what you need to have. But
euodoó—God is going to give you help on the way.

So there's no need to complain that you don't have provision. There's no need to be discouraged like Elijah was and
say, "I'm the only one." God is bringing help on the road to
your promise.

Today declare...

> *I declare victory. I do not need all the answers. I
> don't need to be the smartest or most gifted person
> in the room to be used by You. You will bring help
> just when I need it. Thank You, Lord!*

_____

_____

_____

_____

_____

_____

_____

_____

_____

_____

_____

_____

_____

_____

_____

_____

_____

_____

_____

_____

_____

_____

_____

_____

_____

NOTES

Day 7—Put Your Trust in God and Rejoice!

1.   Kimberly Daniels, *Inside Out* (Lake Mary, FL: Charisma House, 2008).

Day 21—Adonai

1.   "The Hebrew Name for Lord—Adonai," Hebrews for Christians, accessed July 19, 2016, http://www.hebrew4 christians.com/Names_of_G-d/Adonai/adonai.html.

Day 33—Do Not Play With Darkness!

1.   Kate Leonard, "Girl Dies Doing Charlie Demon Challenge Social Craze," The News Nerd, May 28. 2015, accessed September 30, 2016, http://www.thenewsnerd.com/local/girl -dies-doing-charlie-demon-challenge/. "Kids Summoning Demon in New Social Media Craze," CBN News, May 27, 2015, accessed September 30, 2016, http://www1.cbn.com/cbnnews/us/2015 /May/Kids-Summoning-Demon-in-New-Social-Media-Craze.

Day 35—Binding Azazel: The Demon of Transfer

1.   Leonard, "Girl Dies Doing Charlie Demon Challenge Social Craze"; "Kids Summoning Demon in New Social Media Craze," CBN News.

Day 65—Snake Season

1.   University of Arkansas, Fayetteville, "How Snakes Survive Starvation," Science Daily, accessed July 20, 2016, https:// www.sciencedaily.com/releases/2007/08/070824173005.htm.

2.   "Do Snakes Sleep With Their Eyes Open?," Explaining Science, accessed September 21, 2016, http://explainers.nysci .org/post/99834246454/do-snakes-sleep-with-their-eyes-open -people-have.

DAY 76—IT'S TIME FOR A NEW LEVEL OF WARFARE

1.   Anthony Pappone, "The Last Head Hunters, Konyak Tribe Warrior," Bēhance, accessed September 21, 2016, https:// www.behance.net/gallery/8009669/the-last-head-hunters -konyak-tribe-warrior.